The Complete Guide Kodi

EDITORIAL

Editor: David Ludlow
Art Editor: Ian Jackson
Consulting Editor: Robert Irvine
Group Editor: Daniel Booth

MANAGEMENT

Publisher: John Garewal
Operations Director: Robin Ryan
MD of Advertising: Julian Lloyd-Evans
Newstrade Director: David Barker
Chief Operating Officer: Brett Reynolds
Chief Executive: James Tye
Founder: Felix Dennis

Dennis Publishing Ltd, 30 Cleveland Street, London W1T 4JD. Company registered in England.

The Complete Guide KODI ISBN 1-78106-585-3

Printed at Wyndeham Bicester, Oxon

Get all the content you want

Kodi is the most popular media software on the planet for two good reasons: it's free, and it's brilliant. What makes it so brilliant is the range of plug-ins that work with it, expanding the system so that it can play more than just files stored on your local network.

In this book, we'll show you how to use Kodi, how to install it on the most relevant platforms that it supports - from a Windows PC and Raspberry Pi right through to the Amazon Fire Stick and Xbox One. We'll show you how to use a VPN, so that you can use Kodi securely, and anonymously and how to install all the best add-ons so that you can get the most from the software.

It probably hasn't escaped your attention that Kodi has been in the news recently, due to the way that some people use it in a slightly more dubious way. We've got you covered, as we'll also explain why Kodi is perfectly legal and how you can avoid any potential problems with it.

Media streaming shouldn't just be limited to Kodi, though, so in this book we also explain how to unlock restricted content on the internet and access all the videos you want, legally. By the time you get to the end, you'll be an expert user, capable of watching what you want, when you want, all while staying on the right side of the law.

Happy streaming!

David Ludlow, Editor

The Complete Guide to KODI

Contents

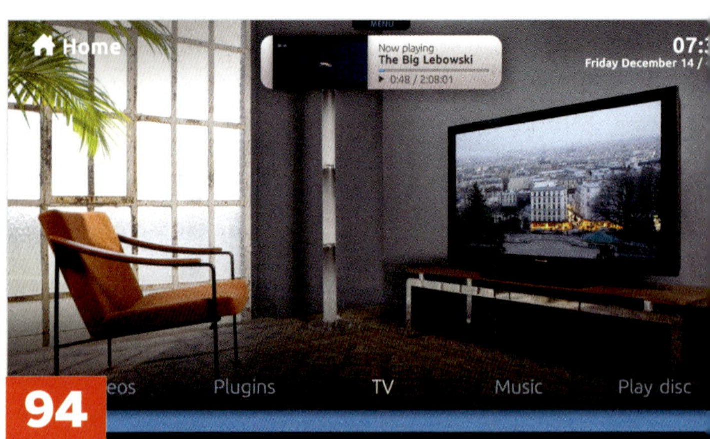

KODI

64

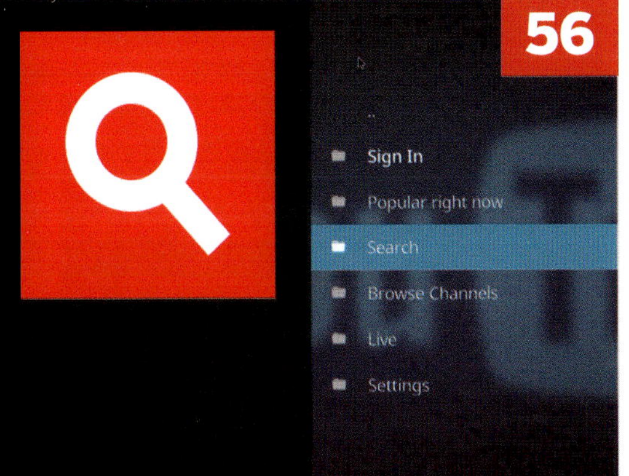
56
Sign In
Popular right now
Search
Browse Channels
Live
Settings

90
BBC
iPlayer

Video add-ons
53

64
Roku 3

Is Kodi legal?

Kodi has hit the headlines for all of the wrong reasons, but we show you what you can and can't legally do with the software

It probably hasn't escaped your attention that Kodi has appeared in the news for the wrong reasons, with the software accused of giving people illegal access to all kinds of premium content, from films to live sports.

This is all rather alarmist, as Kodi itself is completely legal, and there are no penalties for downloading and using it. The bog standard software is just a well-designed media streamer, with an interface that works well on full-screen or a TV.

Kodi is just open-source (read, free) software designed specifically with home entertainment in mind. Although Kodi was created for the Microsoft Xbox and originally called Xbox Media Center (XBMC), the software has continued to evolve, spawning a community of its own. Kodi is managed by the non-profit XBMC Foundation and is continually modified and upgraded by hundreds of coders around the world. Since its creation in 2003, Kodi has been shaped by more than 500 software developers and more than 200 translators.

What does Kodi do?

Kodi essentially turns almost any computer, smartphone or tablet into a digital set-top box or streamer, giving users the ability to stream files from the internet, a home network and local storage. In other words, it's very similar to an Apple TV or even the original Windows Media Center.

Kodi is available on almost every device you can think of. The media centre software is easy to download, and compatible with OS X, Linux, Windows, Android and even the Raspberry Pi microcomputer. For those using iOS, the process is slightly more complicated: iPhone users will need to make sure their phone is jailbroken before downloading it.

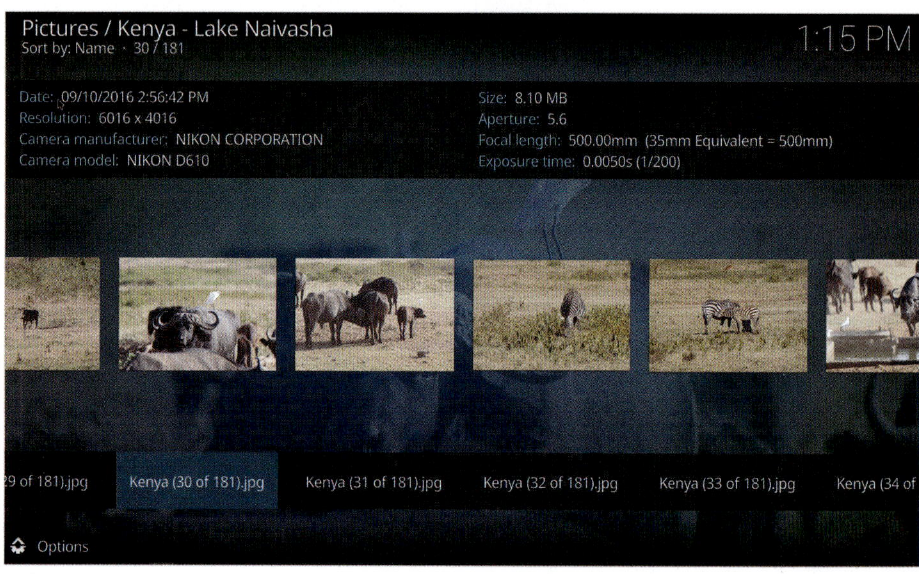

▲ Kodi itself is just software for streaming photos, videos and music

Kodi's purpose-built UI makes browsing through your content simple. The software features what its developers call a "10-foot UI", meaning it can be read from a theoretical distance of up to 10ft away On smaller devices, Kodi offers a similar experience but can be hooked up to a larger TV for big-screen viewing.

Unlike other TV streamers such as the new Apple TV, Chromecast 2 and Amazon Fire TV Stick, Kodi isn't held back by licensing or a curated app store, so it lets you download a range of community-made add-ons, and watch whatever you like.

▲ Kodi's big interface is designed to be used on a TV

Is anything about Kodi illegal?

As developers are free to create their own add-ons for Kodi, several have taken the decision to create plug-ins that stream premium content for free, including the latest movies, TV shows and even live sports. Kodi officially distances itself from these add-ons, but it can't physically stop them being created. It's the same for

▲ There's a crack down on fully loaded Kodi boxes, but sellers, such as Brian Thompson, are saying that they're doing nothing wrong (image credit, Northern Echo)

Windows: Microsoft can't stop people from using software that lets people download illegal content.

The real question should be, are these add-ons illegal? This is actually something of a grey area. Downloading copyrighted material is certainly illegal and enforceable by the Police. However, streaming copyrighted material is something rather different. In a landmark ruling, the Court of Justice of the European Union ruled that internet users that looked at copyrighted materials are not breaking the law. According to the judgement any material that appears "on the user's computer screen" and "in the internet 'cache' of that computer's hard disk" are counted as temporary copies and "may therefore be made without the authorisation of the copyright holders".

In short, then, the ruling suggests that streaming, as an individual, is not illegal, as you only ever store a small temporary copy of the file. The UK's National Trading Standards office is clearer on the matter.

"The law as we see it, as we are advised by our legal people, is that if you are a public house, or club, or a business of that nature, who is illegally accessing this particular content – if you're streaming it, you are committing an offence," Howard Turton, of the National Trading Standards North East Regional Investigations Team, told the Express.co.uk. "If you are Joe public, who has bought one of these boxes, technically you might be committing an offence – but it's very difficult for enforcement bodies to tackle a person in their own home doing this type of thing."

We're not legal experts, so the best advice that we can give you is, if some content seems too good to be true then, at best, it's morally wrong to view it, if not illegal.

The Police are already cracking down on people selling fully loaded Kodi boxes - one that ships with Kodi and all of the dubious add-ons pre-installed. A case is going through court right now, with shop-keeper Brian Thompson charged with two counts of selling equipment that facilitated the circumvention of copyright material, regarding fully-loaded Kodi boxes. Thompson has pleaded not guilty.

"These boxes are available from all over the place, not just me, but it's the downloading of software to watch channels that is apparently causing the problem," Thompson told the Northern Echo. "If I am found guilty and the court rules that I am breaking the law selling these boxes, I want to know what that means for people buying and selling mobile phones or laptops because the software is available for all of them."

The Premier League has also won the right to shut down the servers responsible for streaming live football matches to Kodi boxes. Previously, it was only possible to block individual users' computers, which could easily reconnect to a different stream. In other words, even if the plug-ins aren't illegal, the chances are that you'll get less content in the future as rights holders start to crack down on streams.

▲ The Premier League can now shut down entire streams, rather than targeting individuals

Chapter
1

Installing Kodi

IN THIS SECTION

KODI

How to install Kodi on a Windows PC

Kodi is, arguably, at its most powerful on a Windows PC, where it has the power to do everything. Here's how to get it up and running

Windows is one of the main platforms for Kodi. Thanks to its maturity and simplicity, Windows is also one of the easiest operating systems to install Kodi on, too. Here, we'll show you how to get the latest version and get the software up and running on your computer.

1 Download the software

Go to kodi.tv/download and scroll down. The first Current release section contains the release candidate of the next version of Kodi. This may not be compatible with all add-ons, so continue to scroll down the page to the next Current release section. This section contains the current stable and complete version of Kodi. Once you've made your choice, click the Installer link underneath the Windows logo and the latest installer will be downloaded and saved to your hard disk.

2 Run the installation package

Run the installation package that you downloaded. Windows will pop up

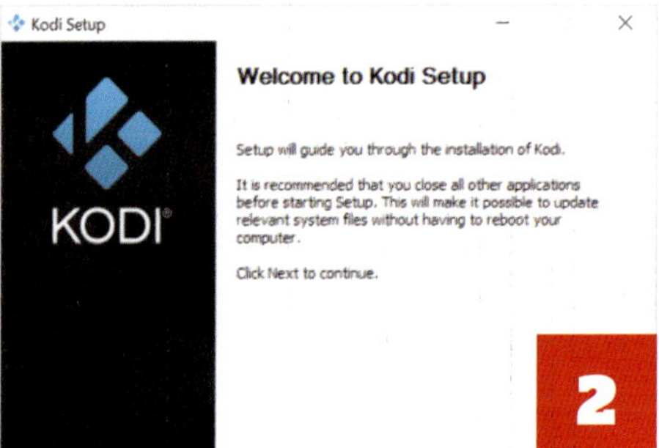

a dialog box asking if you want to run the program, so click the Yes box to continue. Click Next, and then I Agree, and you'll be given a choice as to which Kodi components you want to install. We recommend leaving all of the options installed to give you the best experience, so click Next. Choose an installation folder and click Next to continue, and then click Install to complete the process.

3 Configure initial folders

Once Kodi has finished installing, you can tick the Run Kodi box and click Finish to start the software for the first time. Kodi will start in full-screen mode, taking over your entire monitor (or TV). When the application starts for the very first time, you'll see that the main interface lists the types of content (Movies, TV Shows, Music and so on) on the left. Choosing any content will just display a warning message telling you that 'Your library is currently empty'. This is because Kodi has not been told where your content lives yet, and you need to configure it to do so. We show you how to do all of this in Chapter 2 (see page, 20).

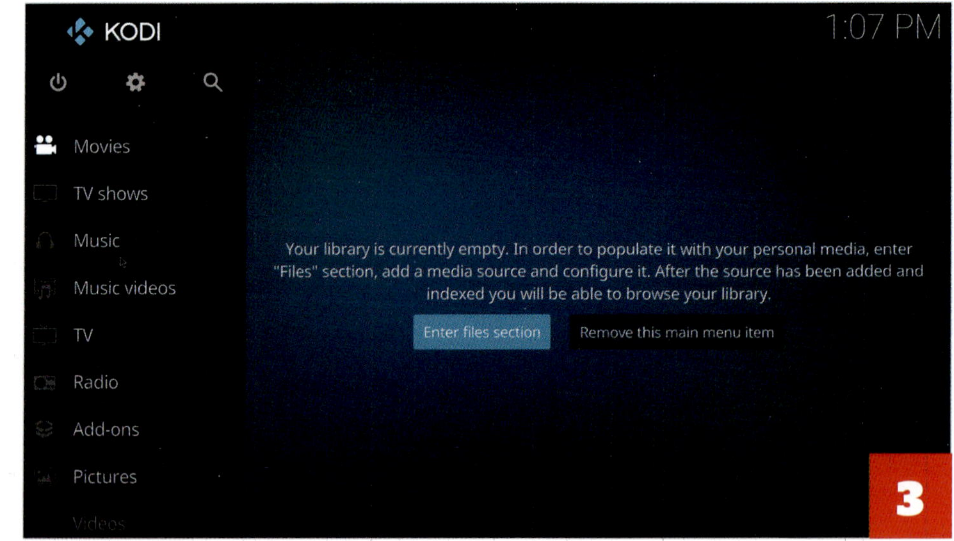

How to install Kodi on a Mac

Kodi works on most operating systems, and you can easily convert your Mac into a media centre by following our guide

Although Kodi may be more commonly used on other platforms, it can easily be installed on a Mac, too. In this article, we'll show you how to download and install the media software on your Mac properly, getting it ready to stream content and download add-ons.

1 Download the software

As with the Windows version, Kodi for Mac can be downloaded from the official website (kodi.tv/download). Scroll down to the first Current release section, and you'll see download links for the current Release Candidate version of Kodi. In our experience, this version is usually stable; if you'd prefer to download the current finalised version, scroll down further to the next Current release section. In both cases, click the Installer link under the Mac version to download the installer .dmg file.

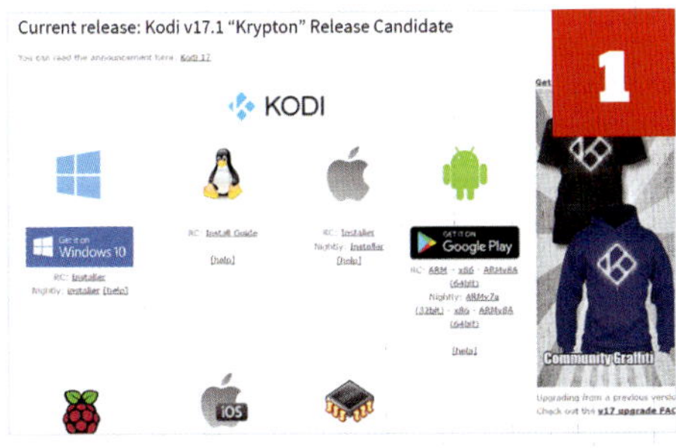

2 Run the installation package

Run the downloaded .dmg image file to open the installation package. In the dialog box that appears, drag the Kodi application into your application folder.

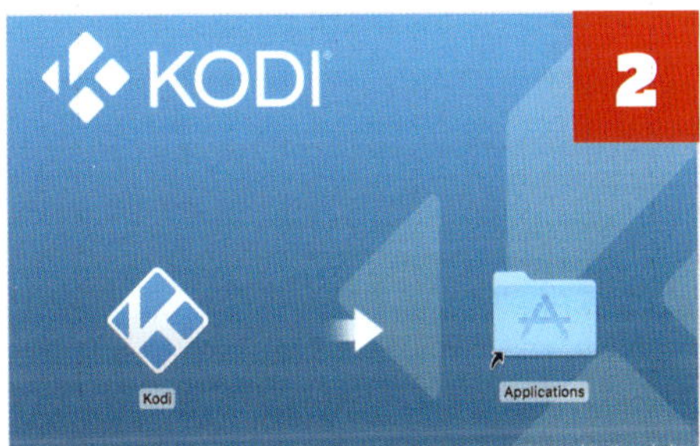

This will copy the Kodi application to your Mac's storage, making it ready to run. Kodi is a fairly big file, so this process can take a little while.

3 Unblock Kodi

When you first try and run Kodi, you'll see an error message telling you that it has been blocked because it's from an unknown developer. To fix this issue, go to System Preferences, Security & Privacy. At the bottom of the page, you'll see a message telling you why Kodi was blocked. Click Open anyway and you'll see yet another warning; click Open again and

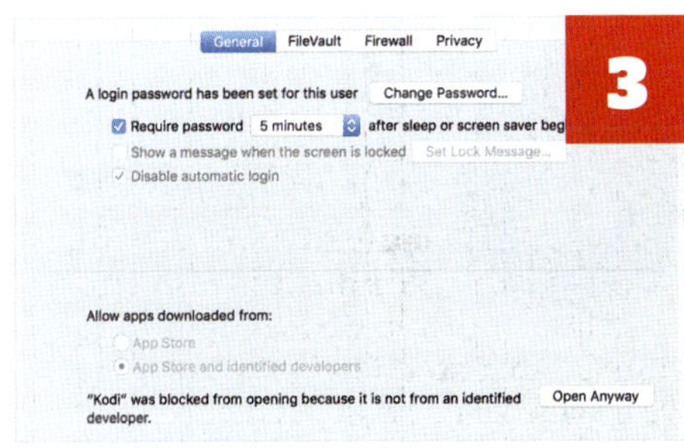

this time Kodi will open, and you'll never have to go through these steps again.

4 Configure initial folders

When the application starts for the very first time, you'll see that the main interface lists the types of content (Movies, TV Shows, Music and so on) on the left. Choosing any content will just display a warning message telling you that 'Your library is currently empty'. This is because Kodi has not been told where your content lives yet, and you need to configure it to do so. We show you how to do all of this in Chapter 2 (see page, 20).

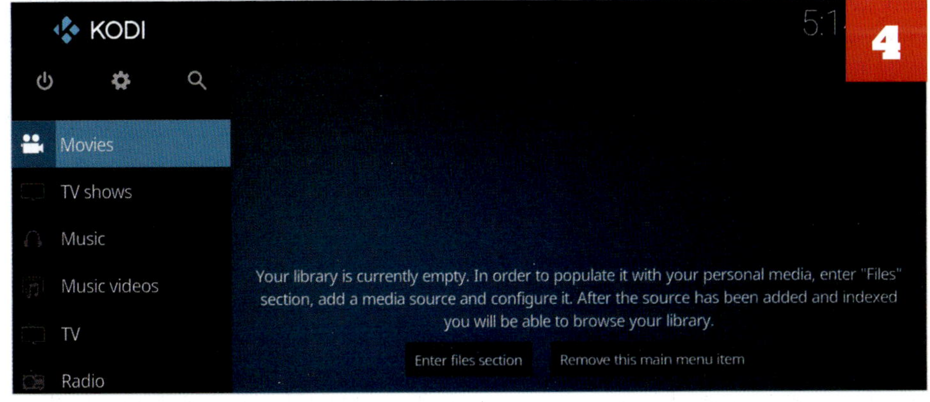

How to install Kodi on the Amazon Fire TV Stick

Amazon's USB-stick-sized media streamer is the perfect home for Kodi - here's how to get the media centre installed

Amazon's Fire TV Stick is a brilliant place for Kodi. This small USB stick plugs into an HDMI port on your TV and is the simplest, cheapest and most convenient way of getting Kodi. Even better, the Fire TV Stick runs a custom version of Android, which means it's compatible with most apps, including Kodi. The downside is that you don't get the normal Google Play Store, and only Amazon's app store, which doesn't have Kodi available in it. Fortunately, it's easy enough to download the Kodi installation files from elsewhere and perform a manual installation. We'll show you how to do this and make a custom launcher for the software, so that you can just double-click the Select button on the remote to launch Kodi. Note that these instructions will also work on other Amazon Fire TV devices, not just the Stick.

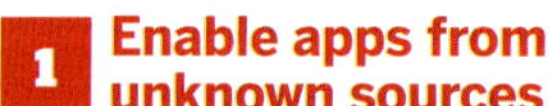

1 Enable apps from unknown sources

Plug your Amazon Fire TV Stick into your TV and plug the USB power cable into a spare USB port or use the power adapter. Go to Settings, System, Developer options. Find Apps from unknown sources, which should be switched Off, and turn it On, then say yes in the pop-up box. Do the same thing for the ADB debugging option, which is in the same menu.

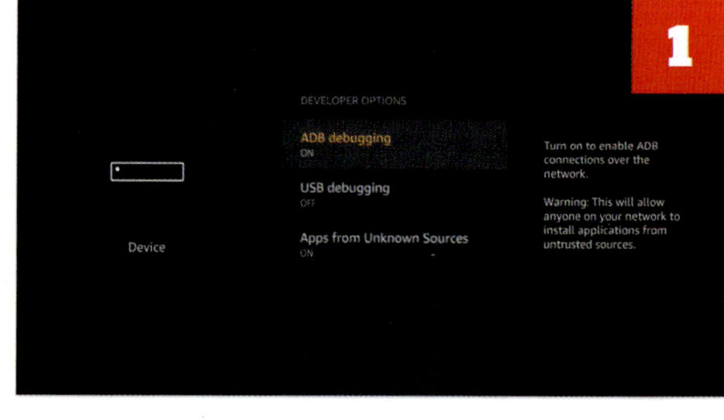

2 Download Kodi

Go back to the homescreen and install ES File Explorer, which will be listed under the Popular Fire TV apps section. Open ES File Explorer, select Favorite and then Add. Enter 'http://kodi.tv/download', and hit Next. The text you've entered will disappear but don't worry. Now, type 'Kodi' into the next box and press Next again, then select Add. Open the Favourite (Kodi) link you've created, which can be found in the left-hand panel.

A website will launch. Find Kodi Android apps and select the ARM version. Nothing will happen, but this is normal. To start the download, navigate to the three dots towards the bottom right of the screen and select 'Open in new Browser'.

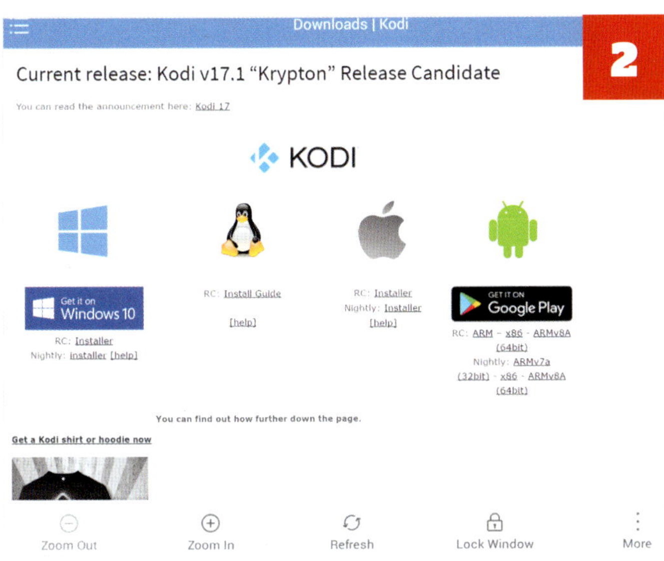

ES File Explorer will then download the latest version of the app to the stick. This can take a little while to do, so be patient: you can something is happening, because you'll get a spinning circle at the top-right of the image.

After a short wait, a Download dialog box will appear. Once Kodi has downloaded, select the Open File option and then Install. A dialog box will open with app permissions, press down on the remote until the options at the bottom highlight, and then select Install again.

3 Install AppStarter

The problem now is that it's a massive pain to run Kodi, as the application is found in Settings, Applications, Manage Installed Applications. For that reason, it's best to make a custom app launcher.

Using AppStarter you can make Kodi launch by simply double-tapping the Home button on your Fire TV remote, which far easier than delving into menus

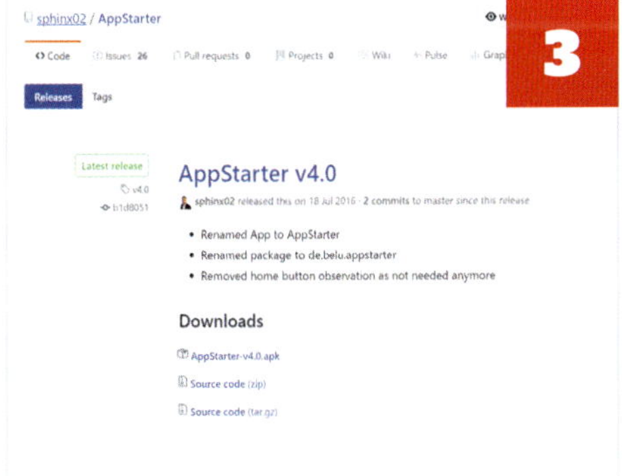

every time.

Add a new Favourite to ES File Explorer, following the same instructions as above, but instead entering http://bit.ly/AppStarter4 into the Path box and firestarter into the Name box. Again, use the directional controller to navigate the web page. You need to select the latest AppStarter APK file but we found this very tricky to do with the controller. If you have the same problem, try moving the highlight over the Fork button in the top-right corner and then pressing down once and you should land on the latest APK file.

As before, download, open and install the APK file to your Fire TV Stick. Click through the app permissions and then choose to Open the app. Otherwise, you can open it from Settings, Applications, Manage Installed Applications.

4 Create home launcher

In AppStarter, go to Settings and select Home Button Single Click Application. Head up the list and select No Action. You can then scroll down to a new option, Home Button Double Click Application. Select that and choose Kodi. Now a double-click on the Home button, from anywhere, will launch Kodi.

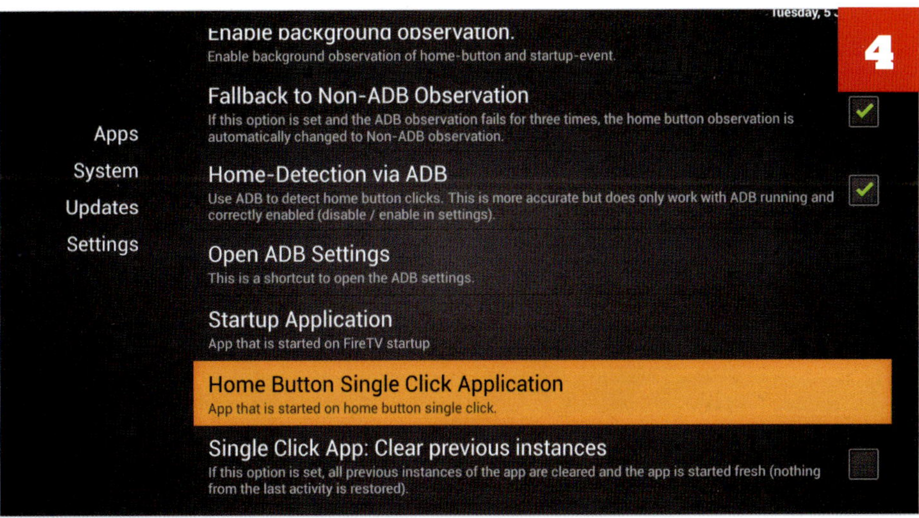

Installing on regular Android

If you've got an Android smartphone or tablet, you're in luck, as you can you just download and install Kodi using Google Play. When you download the software, you'll get the latest stable release of the media software and regular, hassle-free updates. The interface for Android is the same as for the other versions, only you have to tap the screen rather than by using a remote control.

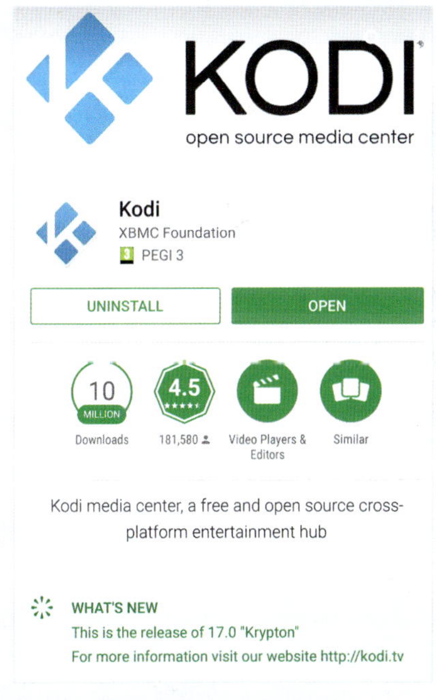

How to install Kodi on the Raspberry Pi 3

The tiny, cheap Raspberry Pi 3 can be turned into an incredibly powerful media server thanks to Kodi. Here's how to get up and running

The Raspberry Pi 3 is one of the best microcomputers around, combining impressive speed with good value in a tiny form factor. It's also versatile too, so it can be used for loads of projects, from making a cat feeder, to a local FM Radio transmitter. However, you can also use a Raspberry Pi 3 with Kodi, one of the best bits of streaming software around, and you'll end up with a speedy, dedicated media centre on the cheap. With nothing more than a Raspberry Pi, a few cables and an open-source Linux distribution, you can network all your media together and display it on your big, shiny flat screen. Interested? Here's how to do it. As well as the Raspberry Pi, you'll need a microSD card. The Raspberry Pi Foundation recommends a minimum of 8GB, but buy more if you want to install media directly onto your media server; we recommend buying a 32GB card at least.

1 Download NOOBs for Pi

If you want to use your Raspberry Pi as a media centre, there are some purpose-built OSes to help you get started. Our favourite is OSMC, a complete OS that comes packaged with Kodi, all optimised for the Pi.

Luckily for those unfamiliar with microSD card flashing, disk images and Linux distros, OSMC is one of the default OS options pre-packaged with the Raspberry Pi Foundation's NOOBS installer (www.raspberrypi.org/downloads/noobs), which automatically configures an SD card with the OS of your choice. To get started, download the NOOBS installer file to your hard disk; it's a 1.1GB file, so it may take a while to download.

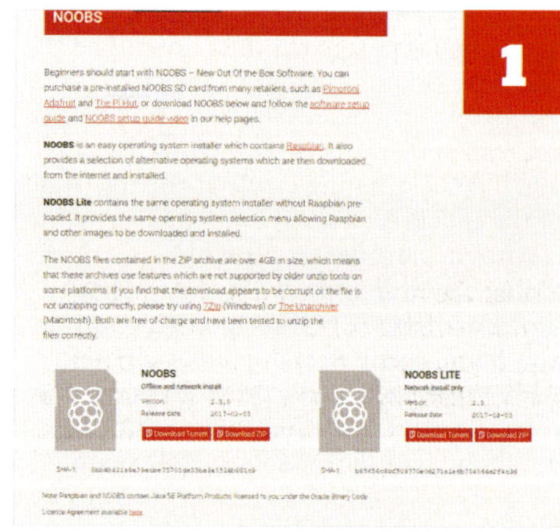

2 Install NOOBS on an SD card

Once you've downloaded the NOOBS zip file, extract the contents. Insert your MicroSD card into your computer, either through an inbuilt port on your PC or an adaptor, and copy the files you just extracted onto the blank card. Once they're done, you're ready to install OSMC on your Raspberry Pi.

If your Raspberry Pi has any problems recognising your MicroSD card, then you may need to repeat this step. This time,

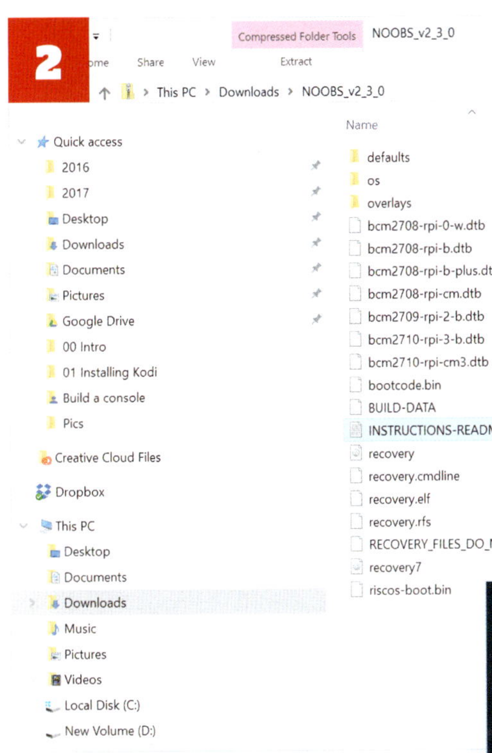

format the memory card using the SD card associations free formatting tool, which you can download for free from www.sdcard.org/downloads/formatter_4/. Once formatted, recopy the NOOBS files.

3 Run NOOBS

Connect your Raspberry Pi up to a display, and plug in a keyboard and mouse. Insert the MicroSD card with NOOBS on it and then attach the power cable to the Pi. When your Pi starts up, you'll see the NOOBS menu. Just select the OSMC option, and the software will be downloaded to your Pi automatically.

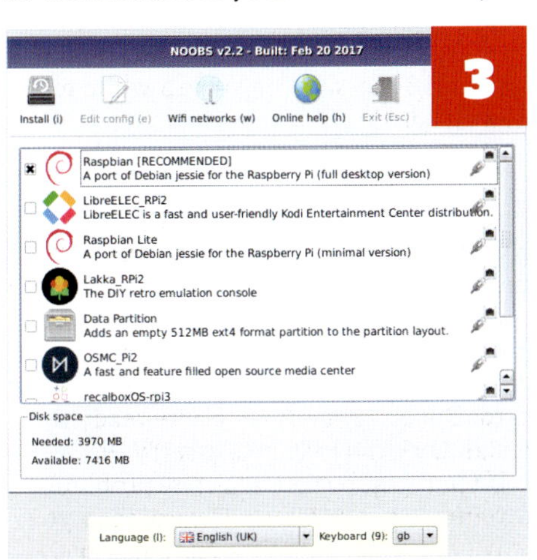

4 Configuring OSMC

When you start OSMC for the first time, you just need to follow the wizard through to set up language, time zone and your initial preferences. You get an option to use the OSMC interface or the Classic Kodi interface. The latter makes a lot of sense, as it will make the other guides in this book easier to follow,

5 Setting up your network

If you're not using a wired Ethernet network connection, you'll need to set up Wi-Fi. Select the My OSMC at the bottom of the main menu, and then select Network. Select Wireless and the select Enable adapter. You can now choose from your list of Wi-Fi networks and join your Pi 3 to your home network.

6 Adding a remote control

The next task is adding a remote control to your Raspberry Pi – no-one wants to have a keyboard and mouse cluttering up their entertainment centre. The good news is that if your TV supports HDMI CEC, your standard TV remote will work just fine with your Pi, and allow you to browse through your content from the comfort of your couch. You can also control the server through a web browser following the steps on page 22.

Chapter
2

How to use Kodi

IN THIS SECTION

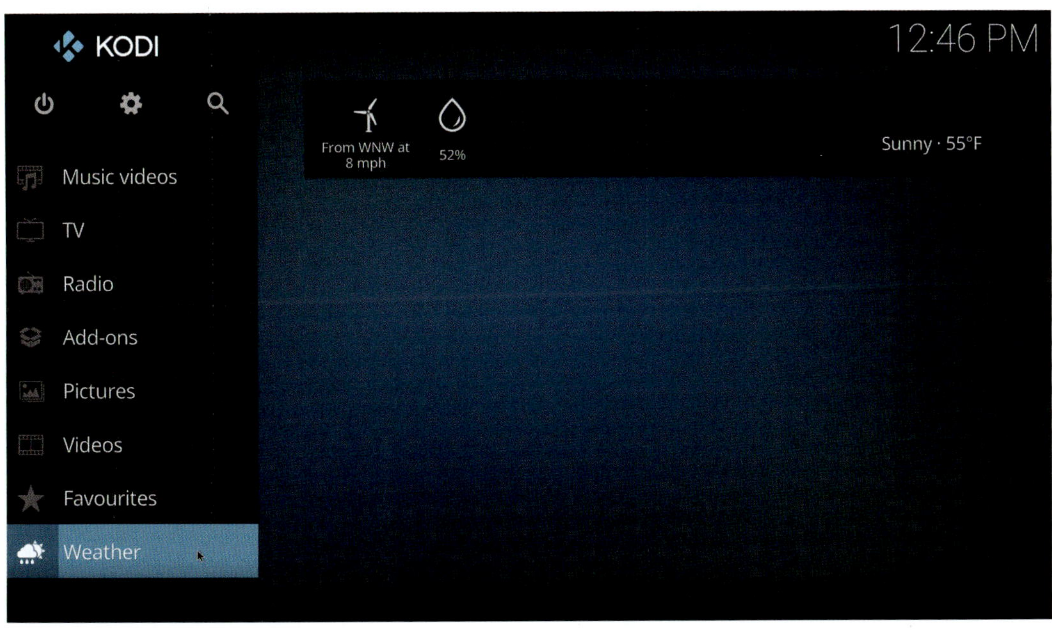

An overview of the Kodi interface

To find the types of content that you want and use Kodi to its max, you need to understand the interface - here's what you need to know

Kodi is designed to be used from a distance on a TV, so the interface is generally very simple to use. This type of interface is usually known as a '10-foot UI', highlighting the distance it is usually used at. However, for first-time users the interface can be a bit tricky to work out what everything does, so follow our guide below to see what all of the options do. You can navigate the menus using your keyboard or mouse, plus you can use the remote from a TV with HDMI CEC, too. Over the next few pages, you'll find further guides on how to control Kodi, including how to use your smartphone as a remote.

1. Power button
Using the power button, you can shut down, restart or put your computer to sleep. You can also quit Kodi.

2. Settings
The Settings menu lets you change everything in your media centre (see next page).

3. Main menu
The main menu gives you access to all types of content that Kodi can stream. It's split into handy sections, including Movies, TV Shows, Music, Music videos, TV, Radio and Pictures.

4. Main window
The main window shows you an overview of your content and more information. Every content section is blank to start with and you can use the buttons to either remove the option from the menu or to add content. See pages 26 to 31 for more information.

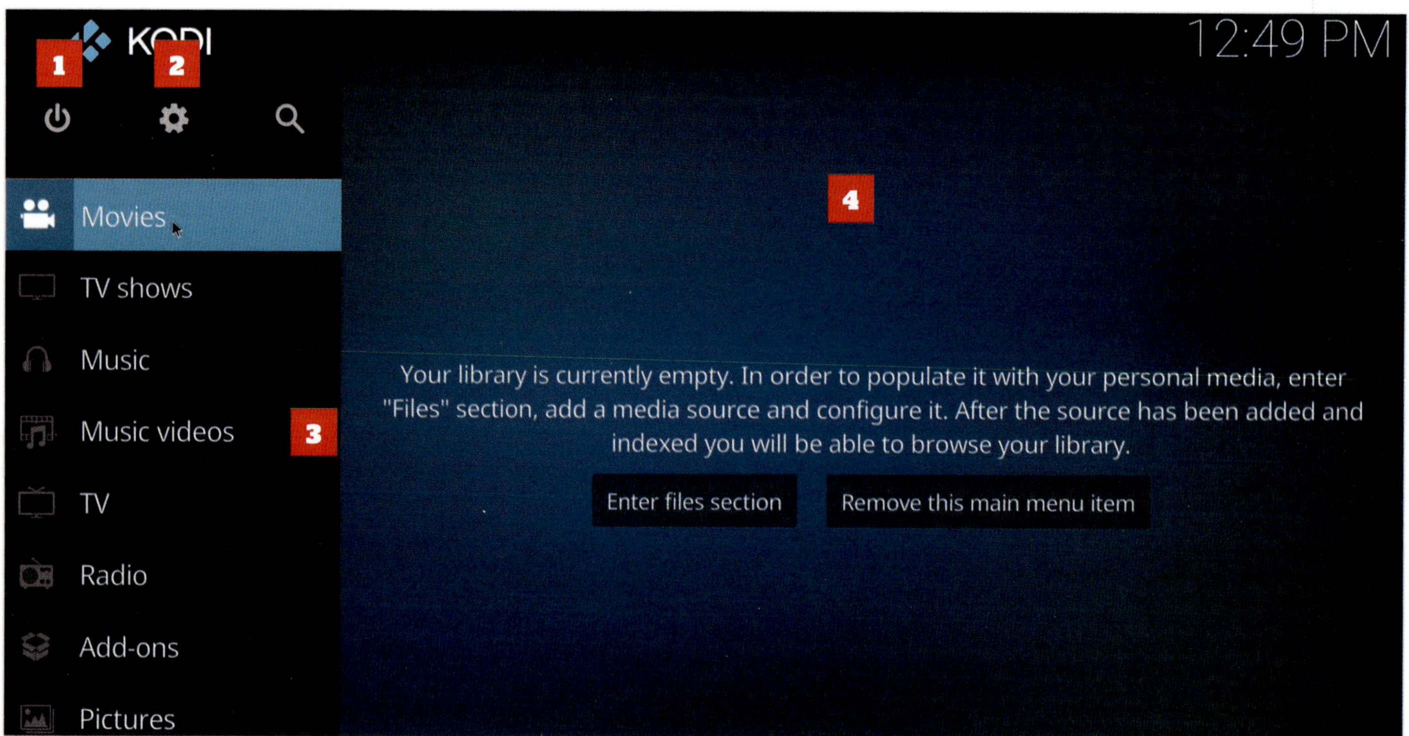

The Kodi Settings menu explained

If you need to make a change to the way that Kodi works, you'll need the Settings menu. Here's an overview of how it works

odi is highly configurable, provided you know which setting to change that is. Once you delve into the main Settings menu, you'll find sub menus for lots of different parts of the system. Here's what all of the options do.

1. Player settings

Use this menu to choose whether to autoplay the next track, how far the skip function should jump in seconds, and everything else to do with media playback.

2. Media settings

You can tell Kodi which folders to look in for media in this menu, plus choose advanced options, such as if you want to automatically generate thumbnail images.

3. PVR & Live TV Settings

This menu is for anyone that has a TV tuner; we recommend buying a dedicated PVR as it will be easier to use.

4. Service settings

You can turn on advanced settings here, including Apple AirPlay and UPnP support, plus you can add a weather channel to get the latest forecasts.

5. Interface settings

Set the interface language and screensaver choice here. You can also set a Master lock, preventing anyone from using your Kodi box unless they have the code.

6. Skin settings

The Skin is the package that controls how Kodi looks and feels. You can change Skins (see page 42), but all settings related to your current Skin, such as enabling/disabling animations, are controlled from here.

7. Profile settings

Kodi supports multiple profiles so that each member of your family can have their custom version of the media player. Manage profiles from this screen.

8 System settings

Control your Kodi box's resolution, audio outputs, power-saving and more options related to hardware here.

9. System information

Select this menu to get an overview of your system, including the amount of memory being used and how much free storage you have left.

10. Event log

You can check important events in this menu, which can be handy if you need to provide troubleshooting information to a Kodi forum online.

11. File manager

You can use the File manager to browse through files physically and to add external repositories for the purpose of adding skins, add-ons and new builds.

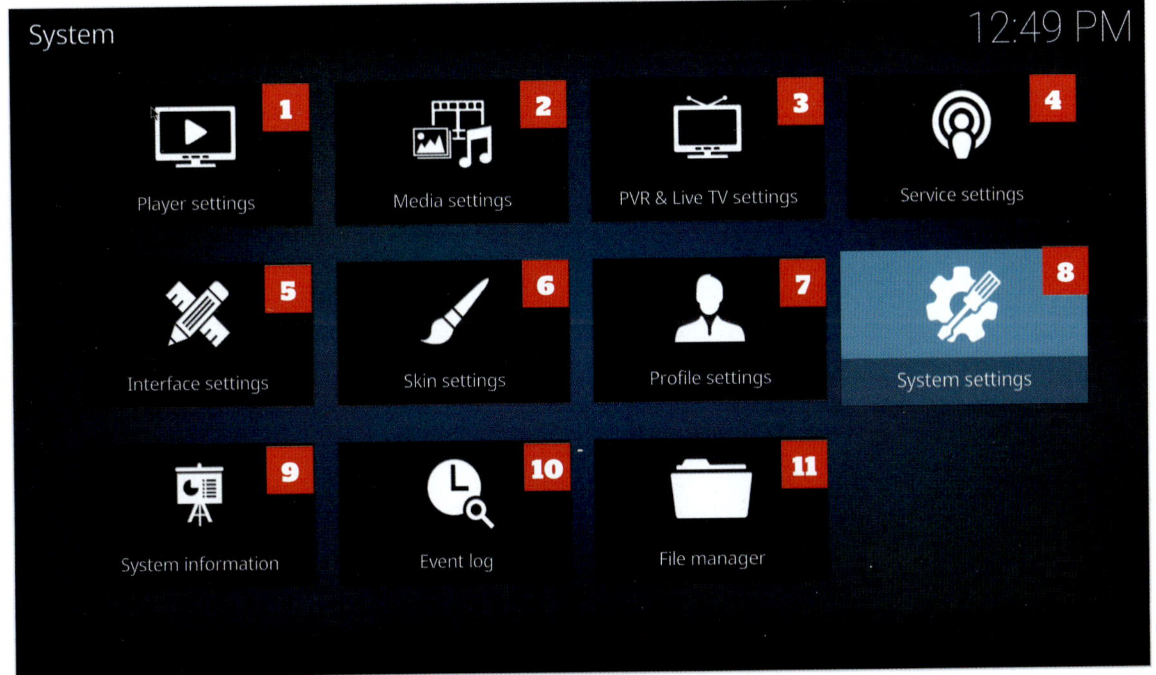

How to control Kodi from a smartphone

Once Kodi's up and running, controlling it from your smartphone is a lot easier than messing around with a keyboard and mouse. Here's how to do it

Kodi's interface might be easy to understand, but it can be annoying using a keyboard and mouse to move through it. So, why not use your smartphone instead? Thanks to the official Kodi Remote control app (Android and iOS), you can control your Kodi box from your phone easily. The only requirements are that your smartphone has to be connected to the same network as your Kodi box, and that your Kodi box has to be powered on.

1 Turn on web control

First, you have to tell your Kodi box to allow remote control requests. Go to Settings, Services and choose the Control option. Turn on the Allow remote control from HTTP option, and the option to Allow remote control from applications on other systems. If you're running security software on your computer, you may need to read its manual to find out how to let Kodi through its firewall.

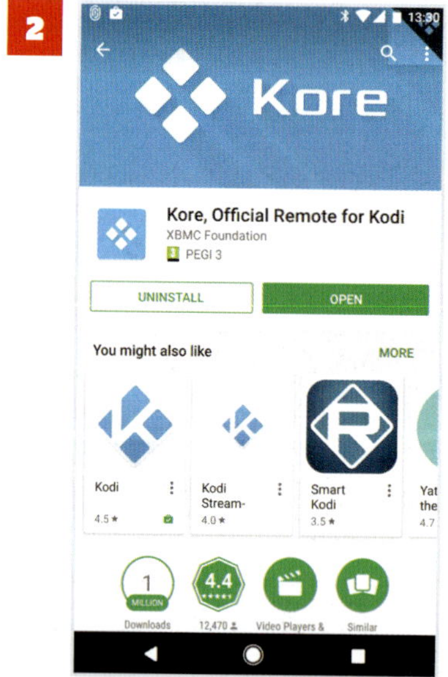

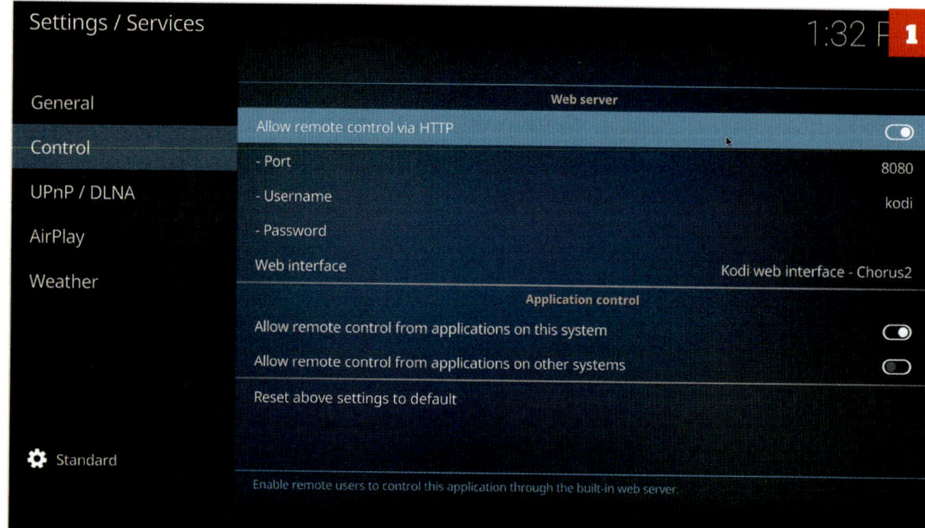

2 Install the official remote

While there are other third-party smartphone remotes, we think that the official one is the best. First, you need to install the remote software using either Google Play or the App Store. Search for 'kodi remote' and select Kore in the search results. Install the software.

3 Find media centers

Fortunately, you don't have to mess around trying to find your Kodi boxes, as the Kore remote control program can automatically scan your network looking for then. Provided your phone and Kodi box are on the same network, the search should only take a few seconds to complete. Once your box has been found, select it and the Kore remote will connect. Tap Finish to complete the setup. If your Kodi box wasn't found, you can tap Next and then manually enter the IP address of your

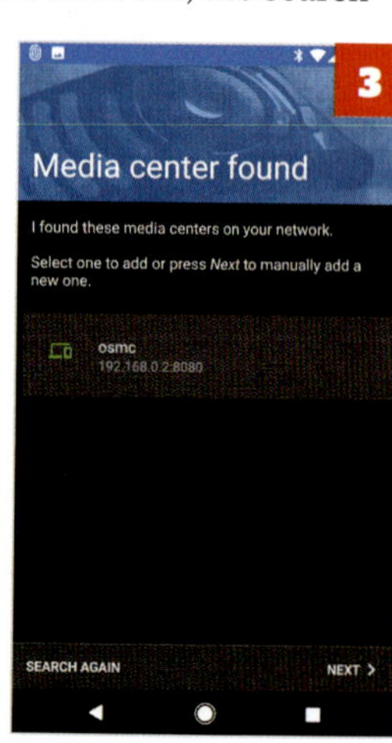

Kodi box: the default port to enter is 8080, and the default username is 'kodi'. If you don't know the IP address, on your Kodi box go to Settings, System info, Summary. Note down the reported IP address of your computer.

4 Use the main controls

Kore displays a touchscreen remote that has the following keys: directional arrows, select, captions, information, back and menu. At the top of the screen you'll get a preview of any media that's currently playing, along with a play/pause button and fast forward/rewind. You can tap these buttons to navigate through the Kodi interface, replacing your keyboard and mouse, or traditional remote control. As Kore operates over your home network, you don't need line-of-sight to make it work, either.

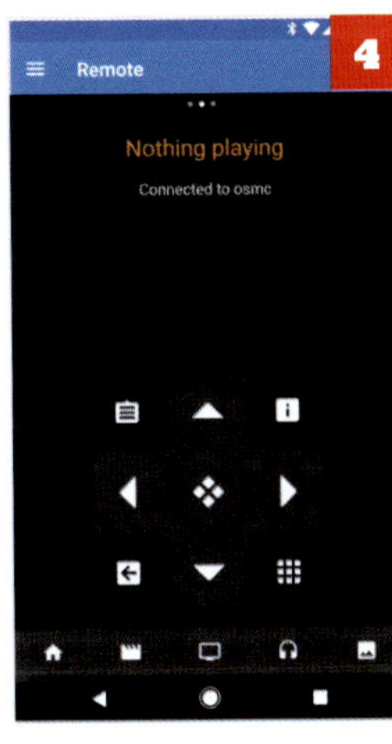

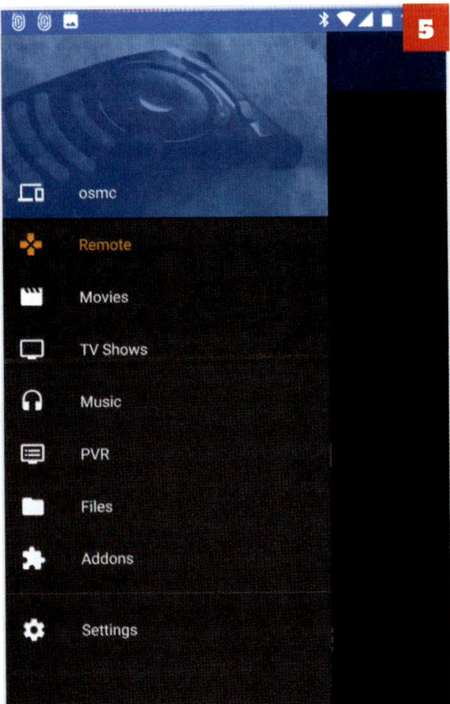

5 Jump to content directly

Kore also apes the main Kodi interface on your smartphone, so you can use the shortcut menu to jump straight to a media section, such as TV Shows, and select the media that you want to play directly from there. This can be a lot quicker than navigating through the Kodi interface and means that you can line up what to watch before you turn on your TV.

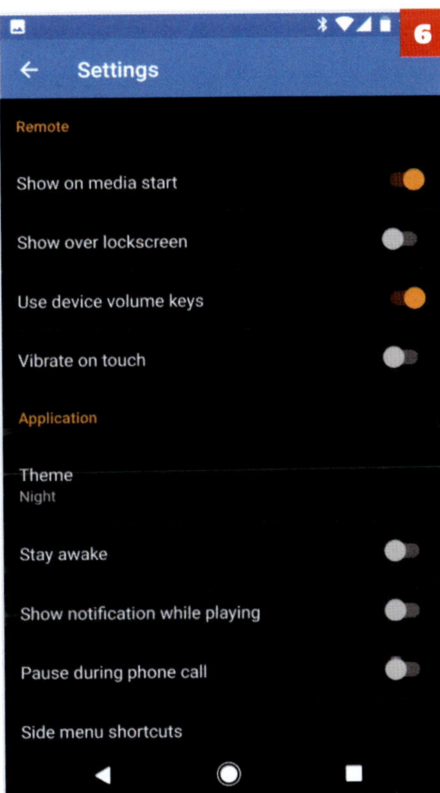

6 Manage settings

Kore has some advanced settings, too. Tap the menu button and select Settings. From this menu, you can choose to use your phone's volume keys to adjust Kodi's volume; you can display playback controls on the lock screen; you can force your phone to stay awake (bad for battery, but easier for control); and you can pause Kodi automatically when a phone call comes in.

7 Manage power settings

Tap the power button in Kore, and you have access to the same functions as if you were sat in front of your Kodi box. From this menu, you can Reboot or Shutdown your Kodi box, but it's better to use the Suspend option, so your box

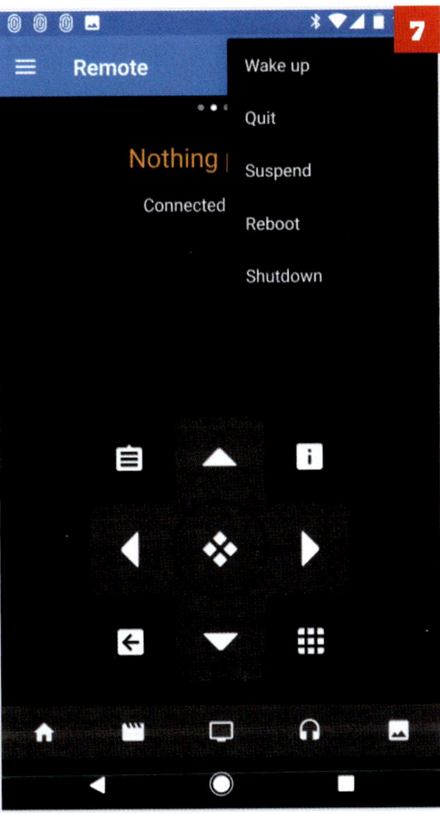

will start again faster. If you use Suspend, you can use Kore's Wake up command to tell your computer to come out of sleep and start up again. This way, you can tuck your Kodi box out of the way and control it entirely from your phone.

8 Switch between Kodi devices

If you've got more than one Kodi box in your house, you can use Kore to control them all. Tap the menu button. At the top of the list, you'll see the name of the Kodi box that you're currently controlling. Tap this to jump to the list of media centers that you have already added to Kore. You can now select the one that you want to control. If you've just installed another Kodi box, tap the Plus icon and follow the wizard through to automatically scan your network for new Kodi boxes.

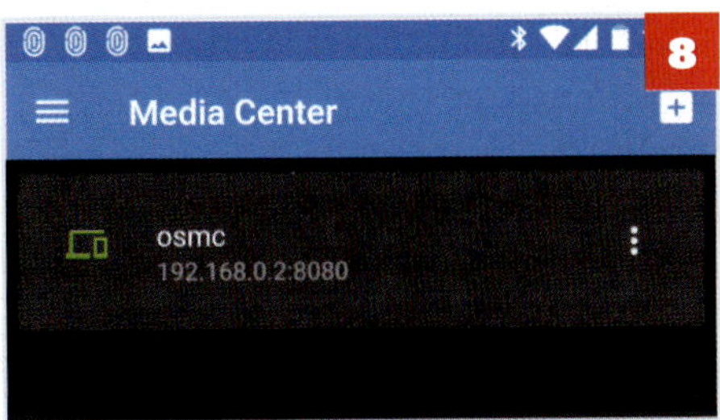

How to Control Kodi from a web browser

Kodi has a fantastic built-in web server so that you can control it remotely from practically any website. Here's how to get started

While the Kodi smartphone app is a great way to get all of the features of a remote control (and a little more), the media software also has a built-in web server. Using this, you can get incredible control over Kodi from any computer that has a web browser.

For example, you can use the local web interface to browse through all of your content, select what to watch or listen to. There's currently no Photos support, but that's the only thing that's missing. From the web browser, what you select to watch is played on your Kodi box. You've got full control over playback, too, using the on-screen controls. Even better, the web interface can send your keyboard commands to Kodi so that you can remote control the box directly using your keyboard.

If you'd rather just watch the content on the computer you're watching, Kodi's web interface supports that, too, live streaming to your PC. In this guide, we'll show you how to set up and configure the web browser, as well as telling you how to get more from it.

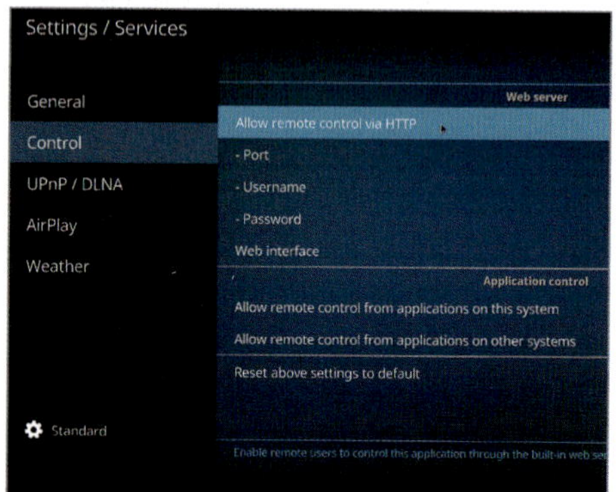

1 Turn on the web server

First, you have to tell Kodi to turn on the web server. To do this, go to Settings, Services, Control. Turn on the Allow remote control via HTTP option. Note down the port (default, 8080) and username (default, kodi), as you'll need these later. You can change both of these settings, although there's little need to do this. More usefully, you may want to add a password for security, so that your Kodi box can only be controlled via an authorised user.

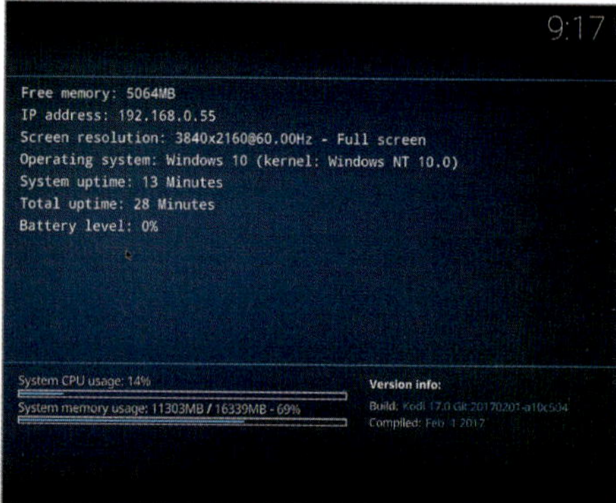

2 Find IP address

Next, you need to find your Kodi box's IP address, so that you can connect to it from another device. The easiest way to do this is to go to Settings, System info, Summary. Note down the reported IP address of your computer.

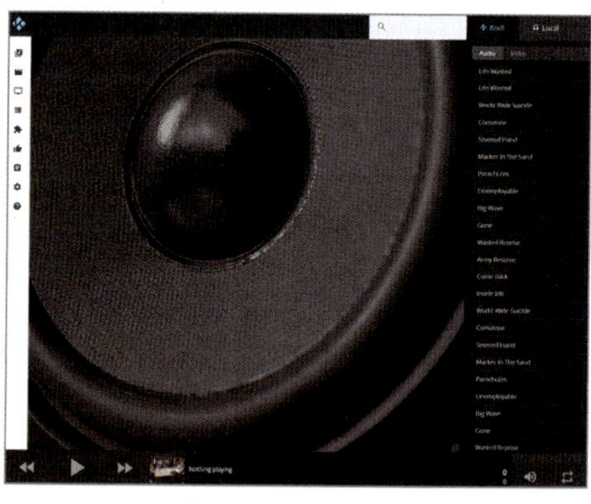

3 Connect to the web server

To connect to the web server, you need a computer on the same network. Fire up a web browser and then go to the following web address, 'http://<kodi_IP_address>:8080'. For example, 'http://192.168.0.55:8080'. Note that the bit after the colon is the port number that you noted down in Step 1. Hit Enter and the web interface will be loaded. If you set a password in Step 1, you'll need to enter this now to continue.

How to use the web interface

Once you've got the web interface working, you can do loads of things to your Kodi box remotely. Here's what you need to know

The main Kodi web interface gives you access to all of your media, bar photos. As it's designed to be used close up, rather than on a TV screen, you get more on display, making it easier to navigate, in our opinion. Using the interface is simple.

Play content

To play any content, just choose a section from the left-hand menu, such as Movies, TV Shows or Music. Once you've selected a section, you'll get a thumbnail view of

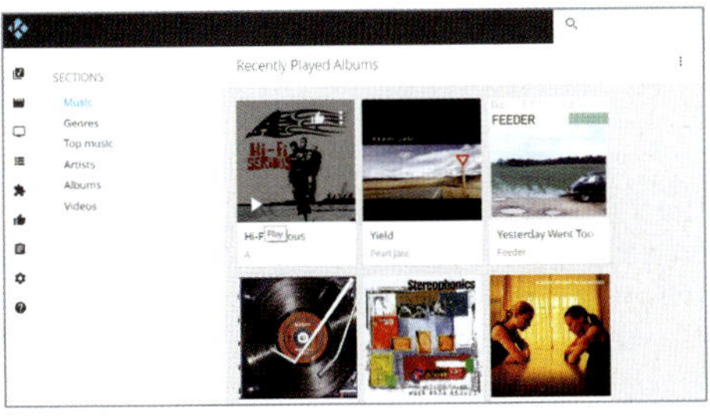

your content, plus further categories to narrow your choice. For example, with Music, you can choose to browse by Genres, Artists, Albums and more.

Hovering over any thumbnail gives you a pop-up play button. Select this, and the content will play immediately on your Kodi box. You can use the playback controls at the bottom of the browser to play/pause, fast forward and rewind through your content.

Get more info

If you click a thumbnail, rather than the play button, you get more information on the bit of content that you've selected. In the case of video, this is a synopsis and more cast details. If you click an album, you get the full track listing, so you can pick which track to play.

Queue content

On the right-hand side of the screen, if you click the Kodi button, you can see the current playback queue, with selectable headers for Audio and Video. Playing an album puts every song into the queue automatically. You can add other audio tracks, or create a video playback queue. Just browse to the content you want and click the Queue button.

Select any item in the queue to play it immediately. You can drag-and-drop queue items to reorder them; hovering over an item and clicking the 'x' icon removes an item from the queue.

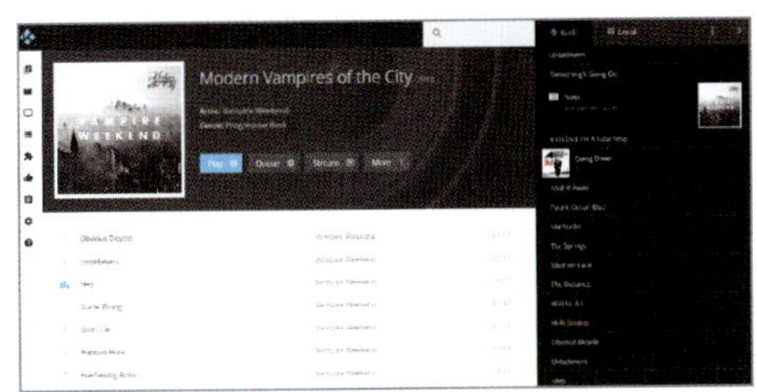

Enable remote control

If you want to control your Kodi box from over the internet, you need to use port forwarding on your router. It's easy to set up for remote control and streaming music; it is not easy to get streaming video working, so we're not covering that here. Before you start, you should set up a password on your Kodi web server, and your Kodi box should have a static (fixed) IP address. You'll also need to know your external IP address or use a dynamic DNS service on your router so that you can

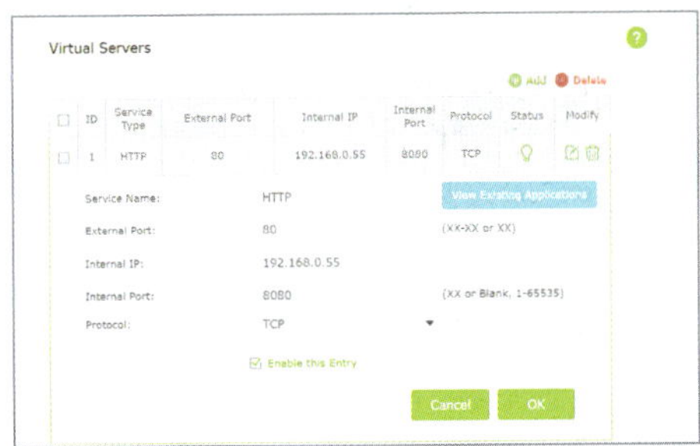

connect to your home remotely.

When you're ready, log in to your router's web management page and look for the port forwarding or virtual servers setting. Add a new rule and set the external port as 80, the internal IP address as the one you use to connect to your Kodi box, and the internal port as 8080, and the protocol as TCP. Using port 80 for the external port means that you don't have to type in the ':8080' bit to connect.

Save your settings. Now, when you're out and about, you can type in your home's IP address or your dynamic DNS address, and you'll be able to access your Kodi box from anywhere in the world.

How to stream and download from Kodi

You don't just have to play content on your Kodi box, as you can stream live to your web browser by following this guide

The Kodi web interface doesn't just give you remote control; it lets you stream content to your device, too. This works best over a local network, although you can open up Kodi to the internet and stream music remotely, too.

1 Stream content

You're not limited to using the web browser interface just to play content on your Kodi box. Instead, you can also stream content from Kodi directly to your device. Just navigate to the content you want to play (audio or video) and then click the Stream button. Kodi will then stream the content directly to your browser. In the case of video content, you'll get a pop-out browser; music is contained inside the main browser, and you can use the main controls to manage playback.

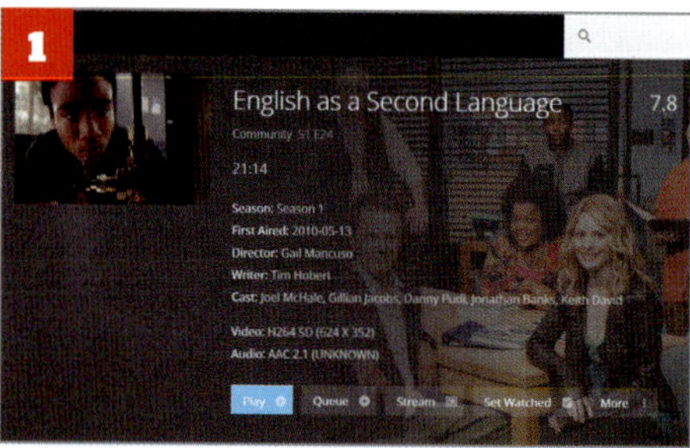

2 Manage a video stream

The default settings for the video stream should work well, but there are a few settings in the pop-out window that you can change. First, you can use the

drop-down menu on the left-hand side of the screen to select the video stream: HTML5 is the default and best option, but you can switch to VLC stream if you're having problems. To go full-screen, click the icon to the right of the remaining time indicator.

3 Download video content

If you're on a slow connection or want to have files for offline use, Kodi's web interface has a download option, too. Just browse to the content that you want to watch. For video files, click the More

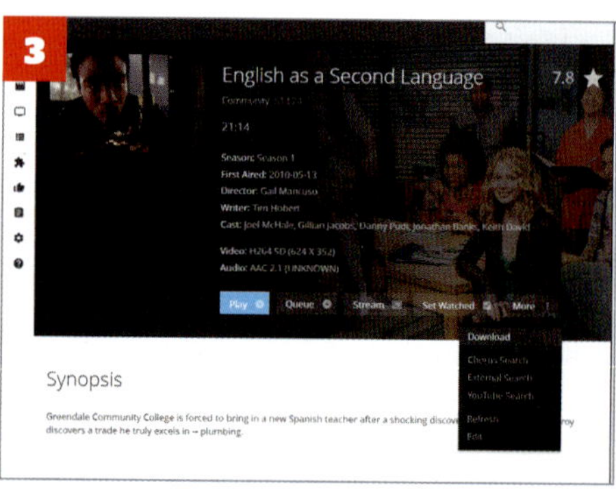

button. Select Download from the menu, and the original file will be saved to your hard disk.

4 Download music

Music downloads work in a slightly different way, and Kodi doesn't provide a method for downloading entire albums. Instead, you can only save individual files to your computer. To do this, browse to the album that you want. Hover over a track, click the three dots ('...') and then select Download song. The original file will be saved to your hard disk.

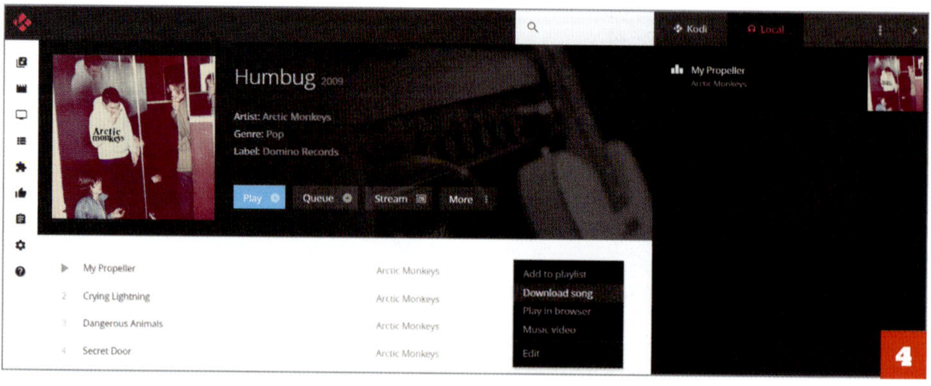

Keyboard shortcuts

If you're using a keyboard to control Kodi, here are the most popular shortcuts you'll need.

The main Kodi web interface gives you access to all of your media, bar photos. As it's designed to be used close up, rather than on a TV screen, you get more on display, making it easier to navigate, in our opinion. Using the interface is simple.

Key	Global	Video playback
F	Fast forward	Fast forward
I	Info	Info
M	"Menu" (sidebar menu on the default skin) Move (File manager)	Player controls (OSD)
P	Play	Play
Q	Queue	
R	Rewind Rename (File manager)	Rewind
S	Shutdown menu	Shutdown menu
T		Toggle subtitles on and off
Ctrl+T		Subtitle position control
U	Move item up (Playlist editor & Favorites window)	
X	Stop	Stop
Space	Pause/Play Current playlist window (video & music listings) Highlight (File manager)w	Pause/Play
←	Left	Seek step backward. 1x 10s, 2x 30s, 3x 1m, 4x 3m... Prev channel group (live TV)
→	Right	Seek step forward. 1x 10s, 2x 30s, 3x 1m, 4x 3m... Next channel group (live TV)
↑	Up	Seek step forward 10min OR Next chapter (videos) Channel up (live TV)
↓	Down	Step back 10min OR Prev chapter (videos) Channel down (live TV)
↵ Enter return	Select	Player controls (OSD)
← Backspace	Back	Back
Esc	Previous menu OR Home screen	Exit full screen
] right bracket		Seek step backward 10min
CTRL+END	Exit Kodi (Only on Home Screen)	
DEL	Delete file (if enabled in settings	Remove from playlist (Playlist editor only)
Home	Jump to the top of the menu (..)	
[numbers] then Return		Jump to that time in playback. (E.g., 1+2+3+4+returnwill jump to 12 minutes and 34 seconds.)
[numbers] then ←		Jump backwards in that amount of time. (E.g., 1+0+ → will jump back 10 seconds.)
[numbers] then →		Jump forward in that amount of time. (E.g., 1+0+ ← will jump forward 10 seconds.)
↑ Shift+LETTER	Jump to that letter in a list	

How to stream any video in Kodi

Kodi can play practically any type of video, making it one of the most powerful media players. Here's how to play local and remote content

odi can play practically any type of media file straight out of the box, whether that file is stored locally or on a server. In this guide, we'll show you how to tell Kodi where your files are located, so that it can start to index them for you.

Kodi works by building up a library of content: you tell it where the files are stored, and the media center software catalogues everything neatly for you. As you add new files into the watched folders, Kodi automatically expands its library sections. As Kodi distinguishes between Movies, TV shows and your own videos, it makes sense to organise different types of videos into different folders first.

1 Manage categories

Kodi has different categories for different types of video, including Movies, TV Shows, Music Videos and plain Videos. Each section is accessible from the main menu. When you first launch Kodi and choose any of these sections, you'll be told that "Your library is currently empty". You get two choices: Enter files section and Remove this main menu item. The first choice lets you tell Kodi where your files are located, the second choice is useful if you want to remove redundant sections that you won't use. First, remove any sections that you don't want, so that you don't have so much clutter.

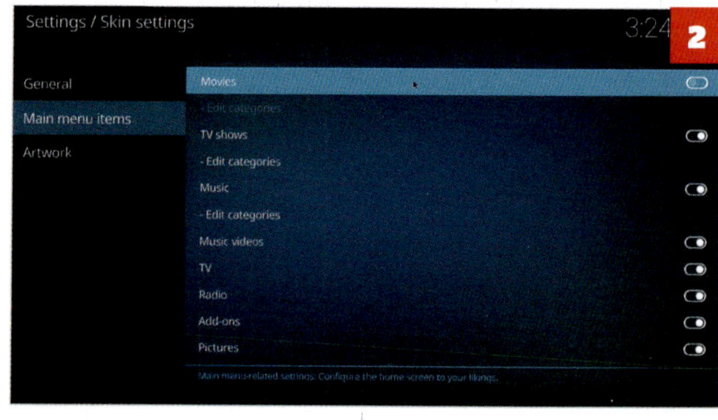

2 Restore locations

If you accidentally remove a section that you do want, go to Settings, Skin settings and select Main Menu items. You can toggle any menu item on or off from here, restoring any that you accidentally removed in Step 1, or that you've subsequently decided that you need.

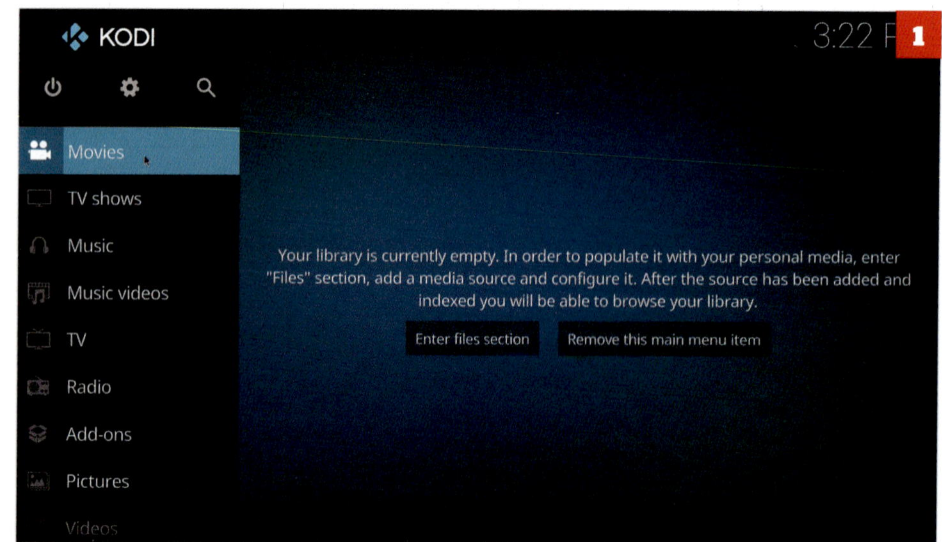

3 Add files and folders

For the menu items that you want to populate select the section in the main menu and then select Enter files section. Select Add videos and then choose Browse. You'll get a list of every type of connection that Kodi can make, including your computer's hard disks, UPnP media servers and network shares.

If Kodi can't see your NAS or other shared folder, select Add network location, type in your device's IP address and select OK. You'll now be able to browse and add network locations.

Select an entry to browse the options, and navigate to a folder that contains the type of videos that you want Kodi to index. Click Add to add the folder into Kodi.

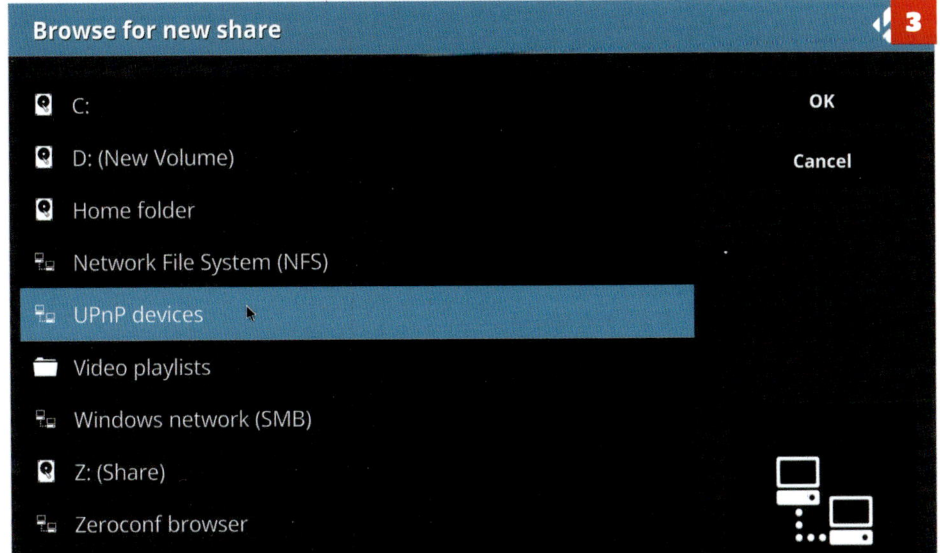

4 Select media type

For all folders that you've added, you're given a new dialog box where you can choose the type of file that you've added: Music, TV Shows, Movies or None. Select the type that matches the folder you've added and then select OK. Click Yes to agree to refresh all content.

Please note that you don't get these options if you add a folder from a UPnP Media Server, as Kodi assumes that the files are organised already. As a result, we recommend using local storage or a network share for all video content

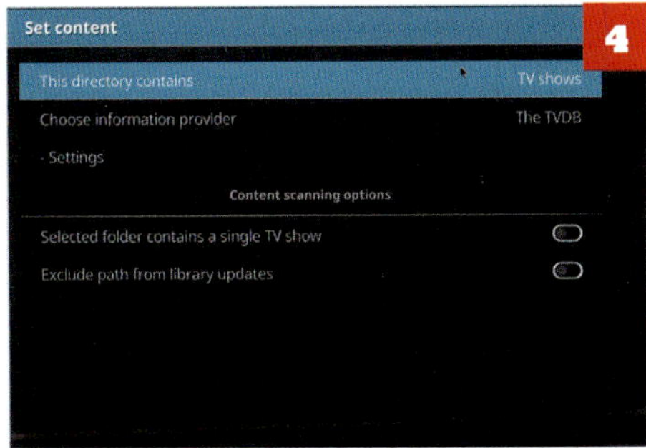

5 Browse videos

It will take Kodi a little while to scan all of the content that you've added, but once it has completed, your main menu items will now be populated. Select TV Shows, for example, and you'll get a list of all TV shows that you have saved, complete with thumbnail views. You can browse by genre, title, year and actors, and Kodi even helpfully shows you a list of your unwatched shows.

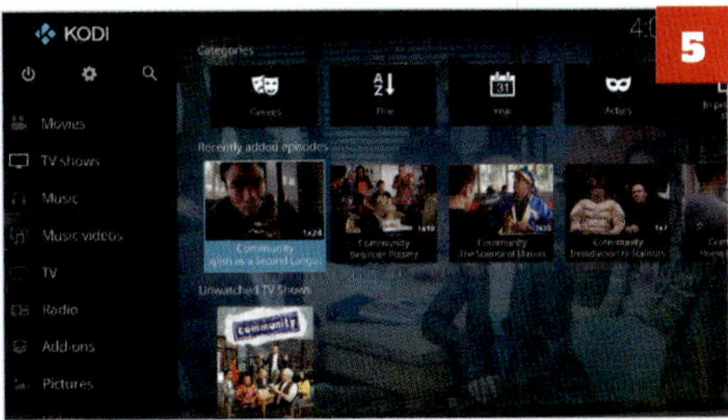

6 Play content

Select any thumbnail, and the related video will start to play automatically. You can use the playback controls in the bar at the bottom of the screen to control playback, and you can hit the 'i' icon to bring up more information about the video that's currently playing.

7 Manage folders

With your main menu items populated, you don't get the shortcut icon to add new folders anymore. To manage folders now, you need to go to Settings, Media Settings and select Videos under Manage Sources. This gets you back to the same interface as in Step 3; just repeat the instructions to add new folders into the mix.

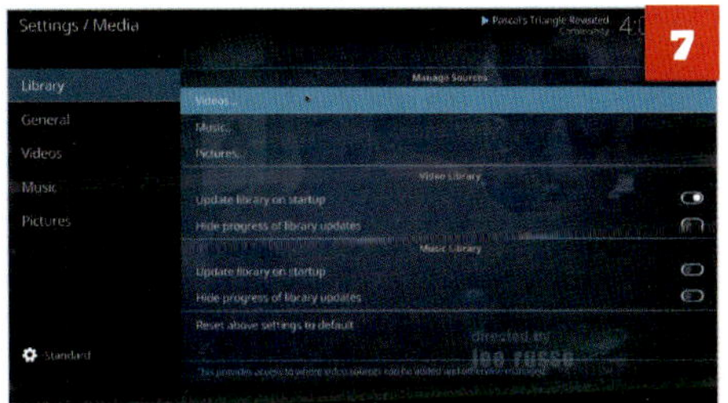

8 Update on startup

To make Kodi more responsive and to update more regularly, we recommend getting the media software to update on launch. To do this, go to Settings, Media Settings and, under the Video Library section, turn on the Update library on startup option.

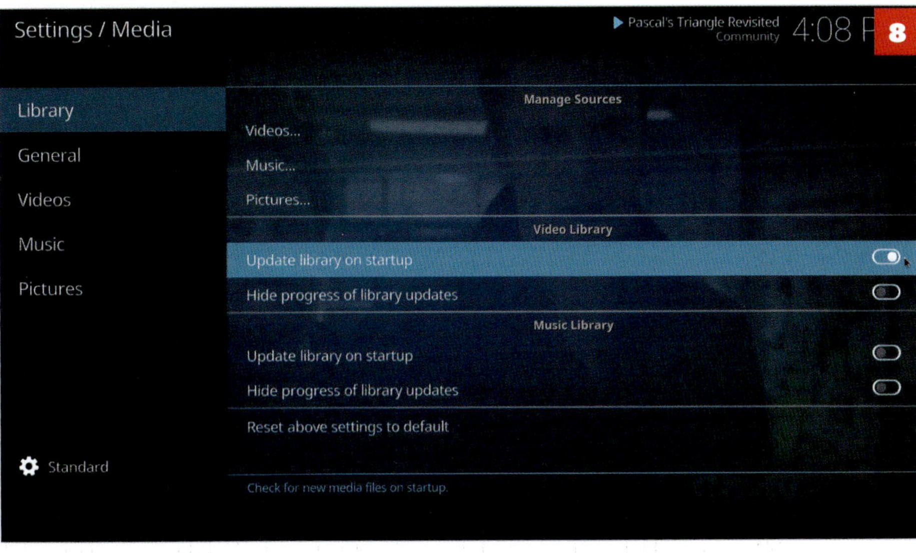

How to stream music in Kodi

Kodi is a powerful music player that can put all of your music into one handy place. Here's how to get it set up

Kodi's powerful media playback extends to music, where it can manage practically any type of file right out of the box. In this guide, we'll show you how to tell Kodi where your music files are stored, so that the media player can index and organise them for you.

Kodi manages music by looking at a set of folders, cataloguing everything in them. As you add new files into your watched set of folders, Kodi automatically updates everything for you.

1 Manage Music

Kodi has one section for Music, which you can access from the program's main menu. When you first select Music, you'll be told that "Your library is currently empty". If you don't want to add any music, choose the Remove this main menu item; if you want to add music files into Kodi, select Enter files section.

2 Restore locations

If you accidentally deleted the Music section, you can add it back by going to Settings, Skin settings and select Main Menu items. You can toggle the Music section, as well as any other main section.

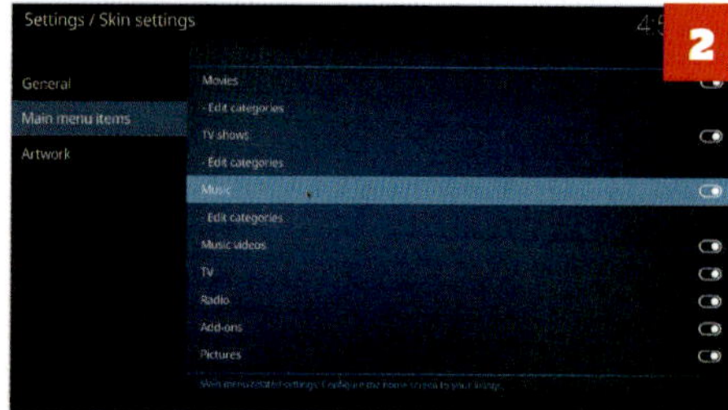

3 Add files and folders

Once you've selected the Enter files section, you can start to add folders into Kodi. Select Files and then Add Music. Select Browse to see all of your local storage, UPnP media servers and network shares. If Kodi can't see your NAS or other shared folder, select Add network location, type in your device's IP address and select OK. You'll now be able to browse and add network locations. Select an entry to browse the options, and navigate to a folder that contains your music. Click Add to add the folder into Kodi.

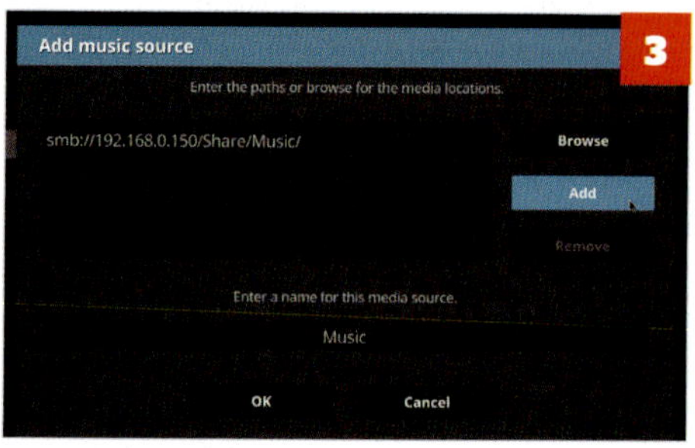

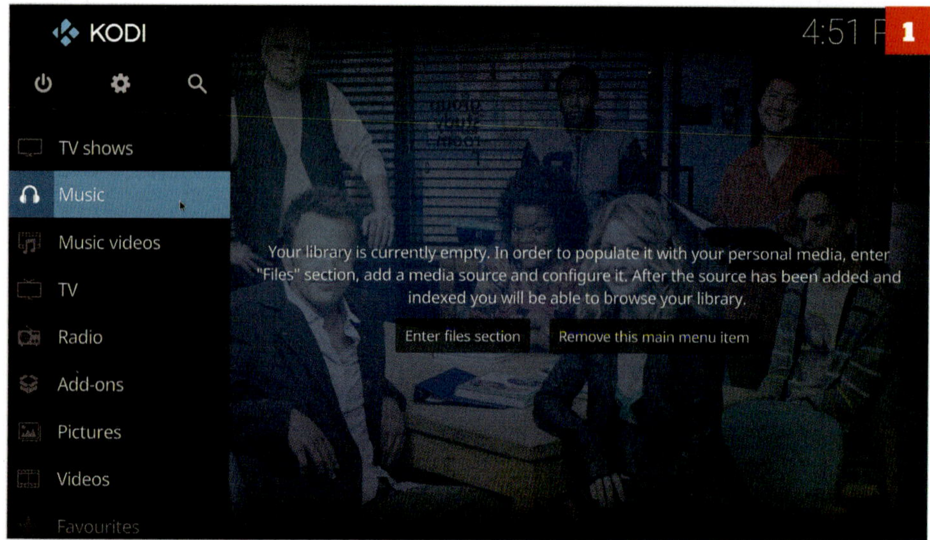

4 Scan files

For all folders that you've added, Kodi will now scan through all of the files and folders, as it tries to identify all of your music. Depending on the size of your media library, and where the files are located, this can take quite a while. Please note that you don't get these scanning options if you add a folder from a UPnP Media Server, as Kodi assumes

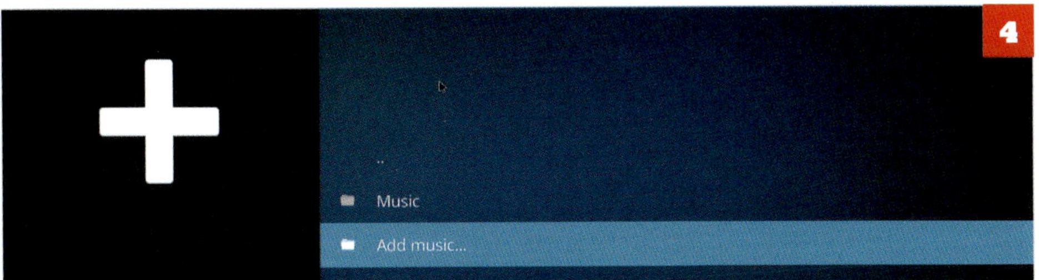

that the files are organised already. As a result, we recommend using local storage or a network share for all music content.

5 Browse music

It will take Kodi a little while to scan all of the content that you've added, but once it has completed, your main menu Music option will now be populated. You'll get a thumbnail view of each album, showing you the album artwork. You can browse by artist, genre, songs and albums, to find the track that you want.

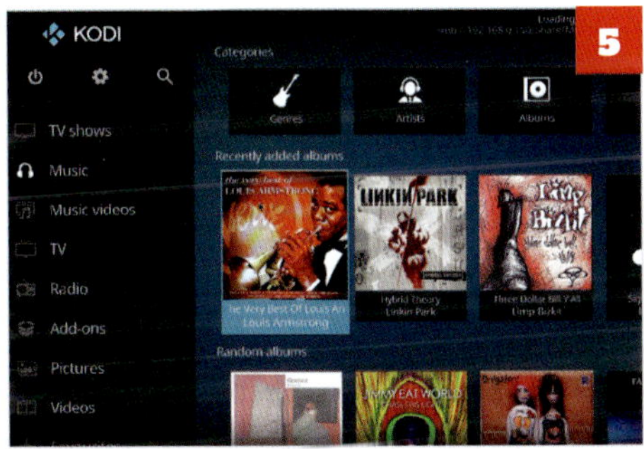

6 Play content

Select any track, and Kodi will start playing it, moving on to the next track automatically. To get full playback controls expand the main menu and click the pop-out button (a square with arrows pointing outwards diagonally). Here, you can play, pause, skip and fast forward your selection.

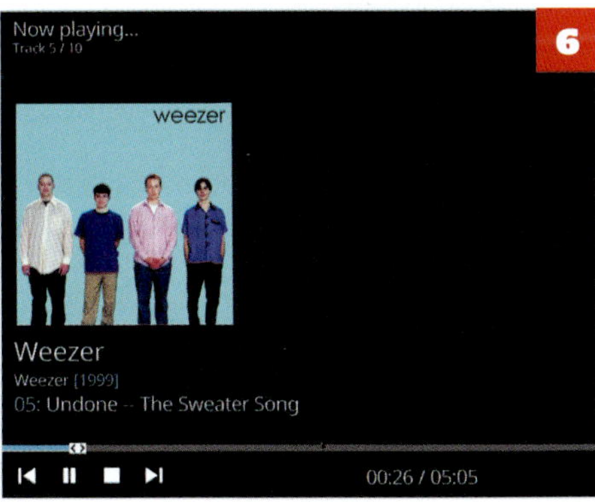

7 Add to playlist

Go to the main menu and select Music, Playlists. From here you can add a new Playlist. Just browse through your library and right-click an item, then select Add to add it to your list. Use the Save option and give you playlist a name to save it for later.

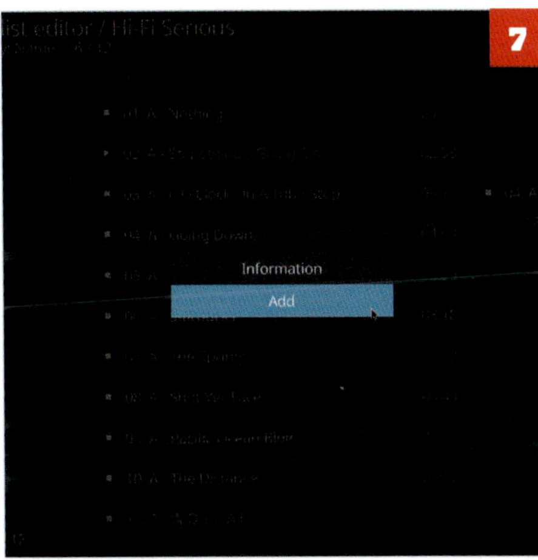

8 Manage folders

With your main menu items populated, you don't get the shortcut icon to add new folders anymore. To manage folders now, you need to go to Settings, Media Settings and select Music under Manage Sources. This gets you back to the same interface as in Step 3; just repeat the instructions to add new folders into the mix.

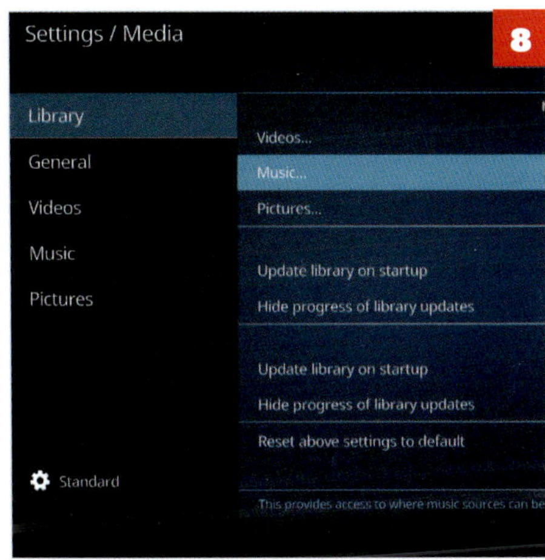

9 Update on startup

To make Kodi more responsive and to update more regularly, we recommend getting the media software to update on launch. To do this, go to Settings, Media Settings and, under the Music Library section, turn on the Update library on startup option.

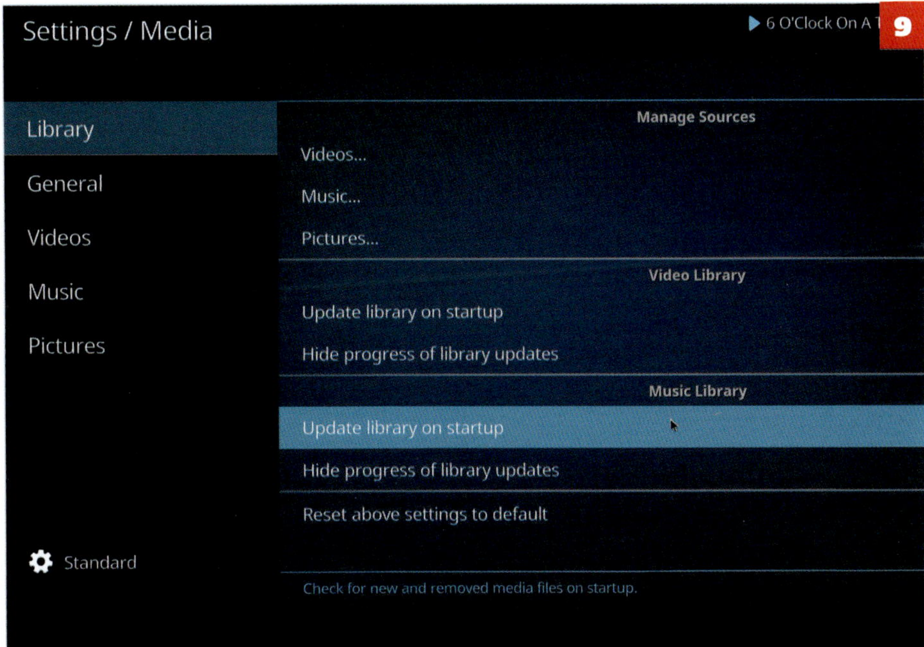

How to stream photos in Kodi

Free all of your photos from hard disks and network storage, and get them displayed on the big screen. Here's how to do it

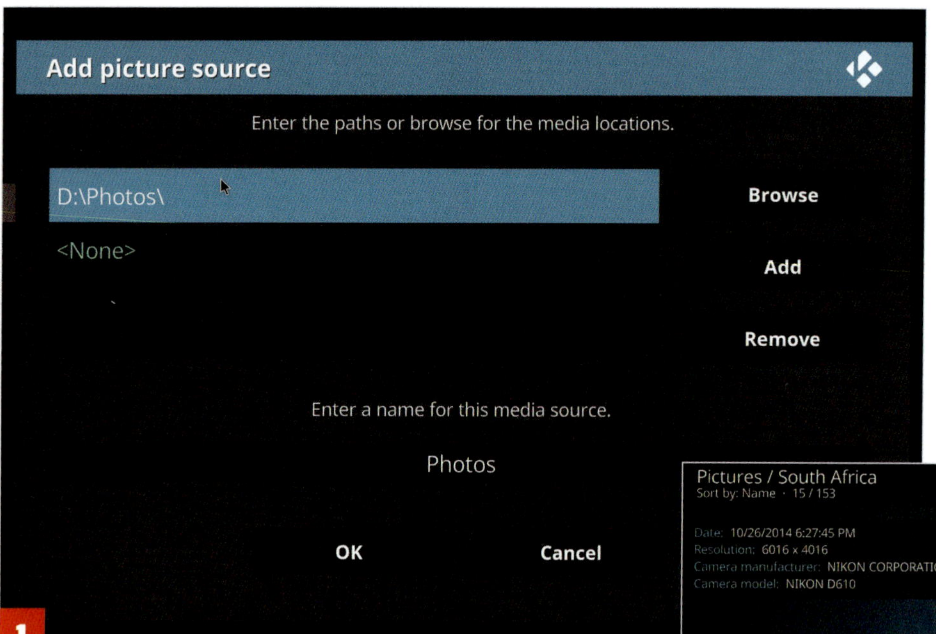

The final main use for Kodi is as a brilliant way to show off your digital photos on the big screen. With most of our collections now digital, this is a brilliant way to get photos off of a hard disk and actually viewed again.

As with videos and music, Kodi lets you add folders full of photos into its library. As you add new photos to these folders, Kodi automatically updates your library, letting you view the new images, too. We'll show you how to add and manage your entire photo collection with Kodi.

1 Add files and folders

Unlike with Videos and Music, Kodi doesn't warn you that your Photo library is empty. So, to add new pictures, select Photos from the main screen and then choose the Add pictures option. You can now start to add folders into Kodi. Select Files and then Add Music. Select Browse to see all of your local storage, UPnP media servers and network shares. If Kodi can't see your NAS or other shared folder, select Add network location, type in your device's IP address and select OK. You'll now be able to browse and add network locations. Select an entry to browse the options, and navigate to a folder that contains your music. Click Add to add the folder into Kodi.

2 Browse folders

Once you've added your folders, you can immediately start to view them. There's no smart organisation or sorting of photos, as Kodi just creates thumbnails and lets you browse them by folder. Just select Photos from the main menu and then choose the folder that you want to view, and any subfolder, too. You'll get a list of thumbnail images to browse, through. Just select any thumbnail image to view it full-screen.

Pictures / South Africa
Sort by: Name · 15 / 153
Date: 10/26/2014 6:27:45 PM
Resolution: 6016 x 4016
Camera manufacturer: NIKON CORPORATION
Camera model: NIKON D610
Size: 12.20 MB
Aperture: 6.3
Focal length: 500.00mm (35mm Equivalent = 500mm)
Exposure time: 0.0040s (1/250)
0309.jpg
DSC0322.jpg
_DSC0324.jpg
_DSC0326.jpg
_DSC0331.jpg
Options
2

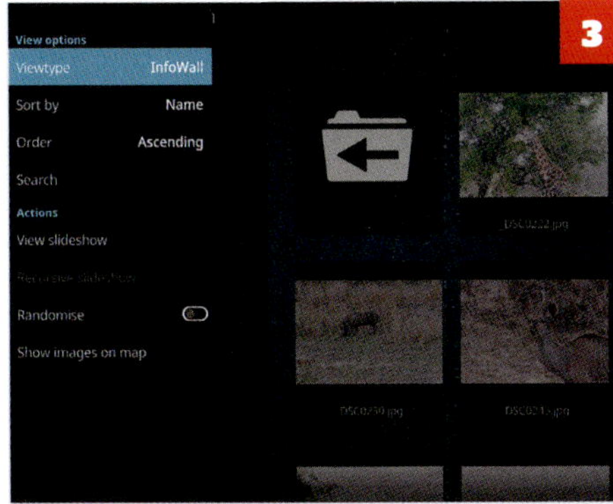

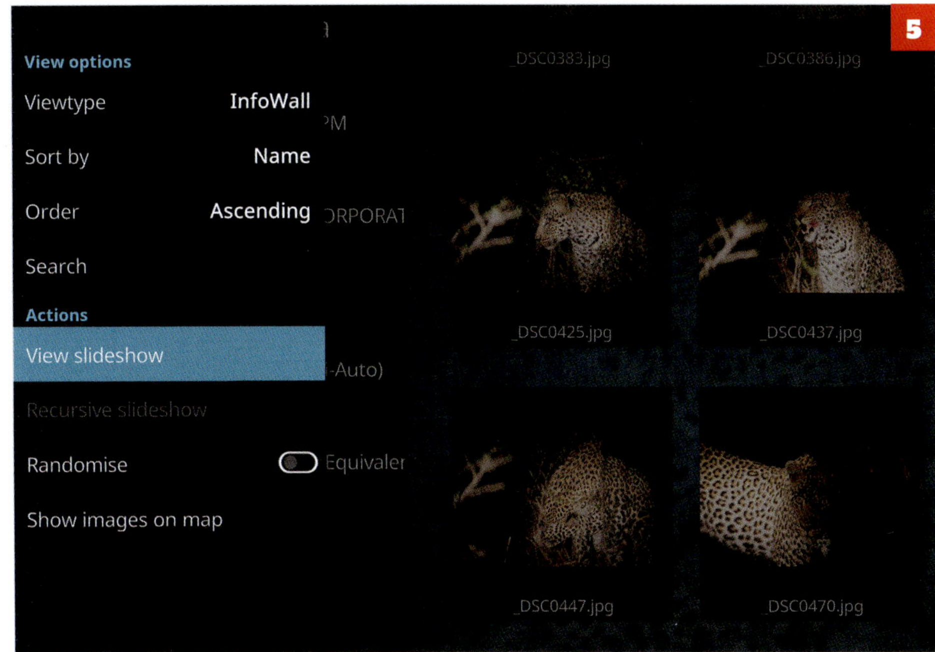

3 Change thumbnail view

That's not to say that you can't do anything clever with the Photos. When you're in a folder, choose Options (it appears at the bottom of the screen, but you can also press the left arrow until a menu pops out). From here you can change the Viewtype. Infowall is our favourite, as you see more thumbnails on screen at once, and selecting an image gives you more information, including the camera that was used and the location if available.

4 Zoom into a photo

Kodi isn't a photo editor, but you can you perform some simple tasks with it. If you want to get more detail in an image, you can use the number keys (1-9) to zoom in; pressing 0 zooms back out and makes the photo fit on the screen again. Once zoomed in, use the cursor keys to move around the image.

If an image has come in at the wrong orientation, tap Enter to rotate the image by 90-degrees; you can keep tapping until you get the image the way you want it.

5 View a slideshow

Kodi can automatically create a slideshow of your photos, too. From any folder, open up the Options menu and then select View slideshow. You can also open any photo to view it and tap the Spacebar to jump into slideshow mode from that point.

6 View photos on a map

If you want to view where your photos were taken, Kodi can do that, provided that the images still have embedded image locations. Open the Options menu and select View photos on a map. You'll get a dialog box telling you that this requires an add-on to be installed, so select Yes.

Kodi will then automatically download the Maps Browser add-on and install it on your computer. After that, you can use the option to view a map, complete with red pins that show you where an image was taken. You can even search by location if you want to see all of the photos that you took in a particular place.

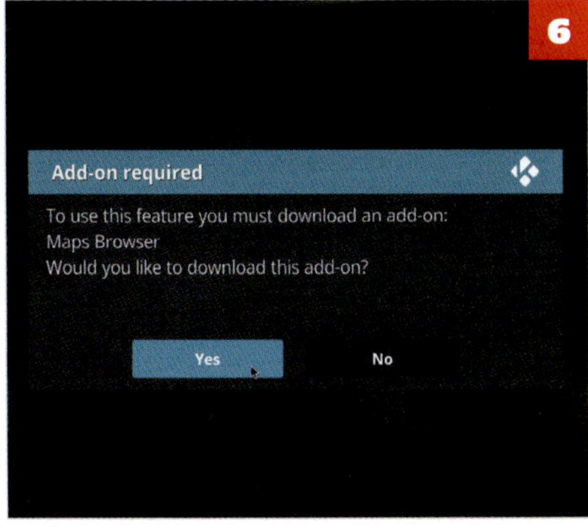

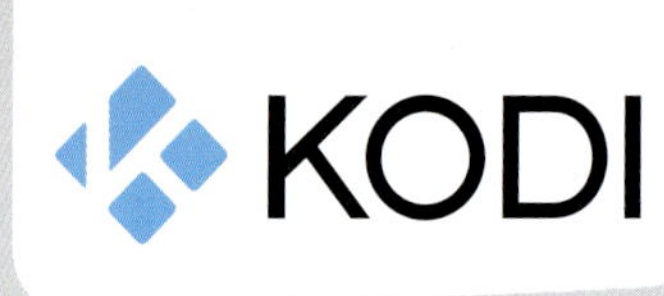

How to cast YouTube videos to Kodi

Kodi is a fantastic open-source media player packed with tools. You can cast videos to it from YouTube, just as you would to a Chromecast

Kodi can play all sorts of media, including videos, music files, DVDs and photo slideshows. It can also stream content over the internet. Thanks to support for add-ons you can expand the software's built-in tools and do even more with it. One clever trick is to cast – that is, send – videos from your phone or tablet to Kodi, so you can enjoy them on a bigger screen, whether it's a computer monitor or a large TV. All you need is a PC running Kodi connected to the screen you want to use.

For this workshop we'll show you how to do this using Pushbullet (www.pushbullet.com) to send the videos. The beauty of Pushbullet is that once you've set it up, it can be used in any app or browser, and unlike most other similar options it's

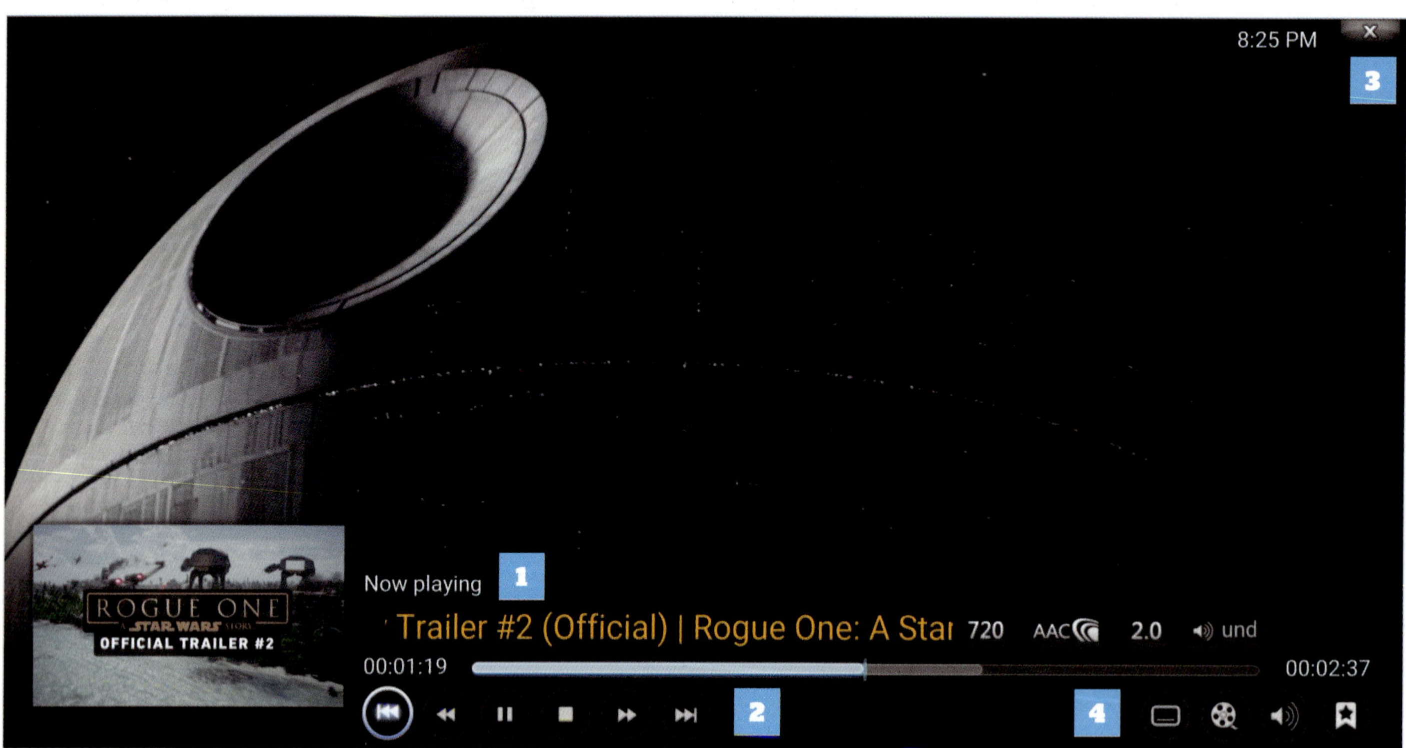

1. NOW PLAYING

When something is playing, move your mouse to show details about the video, such as its name, duration, and resolution

2. CONTROLS

You stop, pause, fast forward or rewind the video here, rather than on your mobile device

3. CLOSE

Click the X while a video is playing and you'll be taken to the previous menu screen. The video will continue to play in the background

4. MENU

The icons buttons let you download subtitles (if configured), open video settings, audio settings, and bookmark the video

1 Enable the web server

Install Kodi on your PC and run it. Go to System, Settings, Services and select Web server. Enable Allow remote control via HTTP by clicking on the button on the right. Leave the port setting as 8080. You can enter a username and password, but it's entirely optional.

Now change Remote control option. Allow remote control by programs on this system should be on, but if it isn't, enable it now. Next enable Allow remote control by programs on other systems. Go back to the Settings menu and select System info, and make make a note of your Kodi box's IP address.

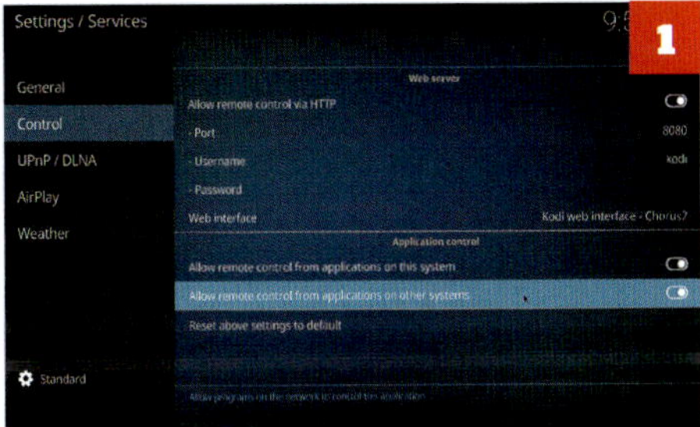

2 Install Pushbullet

There are several ways to cast videos from your mobile device to Kodi, but one of the best options is Pushbullet. Install the app on your mobile device, run it, and sign in with either Facebook or Google. Grant the app the required permissions if installing in Android.

3 Configure Kodi to receive content

You now need to configure Kodi to receive content from Pushbullet. Go to System, Settings, Add-ons and select Install from repository. Select Services, then scroll down the list to Pushbullet. Select it and click the Install button. When done, click the Home button and go to Programs. Click Pushbullet.

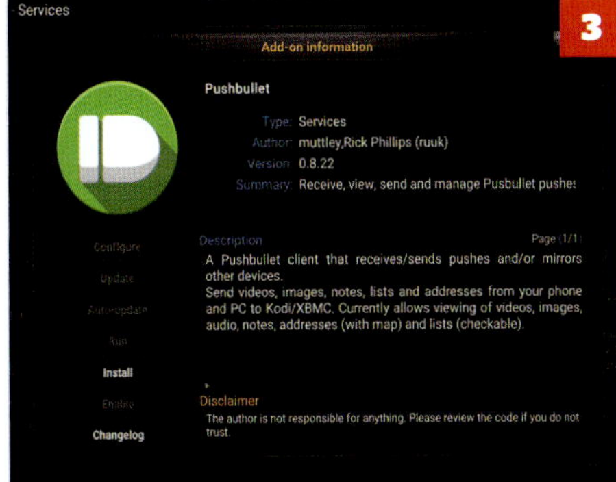

4 Authorise your devices

Click Authorize. A message appears on screen. On your mobile device, open your web browser and go to auth.2ndmind.com. Enter the code and complete the authorisation by signing into Google or Facebook again. Allow the permissions for Pushbullet, and then click the Approve button. Back in Kodi, an 'Authorization complete' message appears.

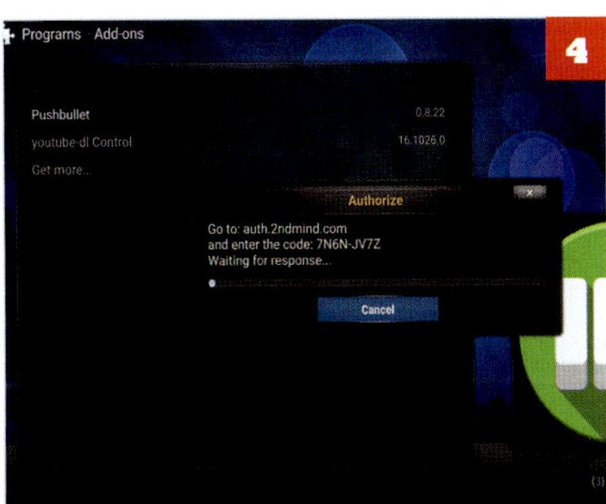

5 Complete configuration

Still in Kodi, click Add as new, type in a name for the device, and click Done. Kodi is now all set up and ready to receive notifications, and – more importantly – YouTube videos from your mobile device. The exact casting process from here will vary slightly depending if you're using Android or iOS.

6 Run YouTube

Open the YouTube app on your mobile device and find a video you want to cast. Click the Share button at the top of the screen and you will see Pushbullet shown in the sharing options. Tap this and Pushbullet opens. Kodi should be listed there. Tap its name to cast the video.

Share

Copy link Hangouts Gmail

7 Install YouTube Kodi add-on

Back in Kodi a message pops-up stating that you need an add-on for YouTube in order for the casting to work. Click on Yes and the add-on (youtube-dl Control) will install. You can also get this from Programs, Get more. Now when you send video links to Kodi via Pushbullet they will play.

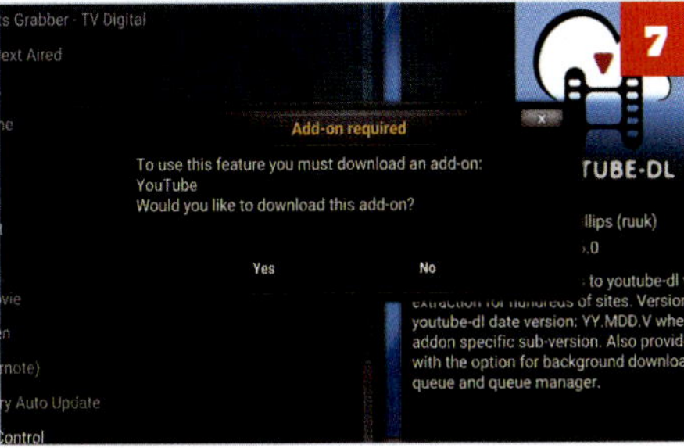

Chapter
3

Expanding Kodi

IN THIS SECTION

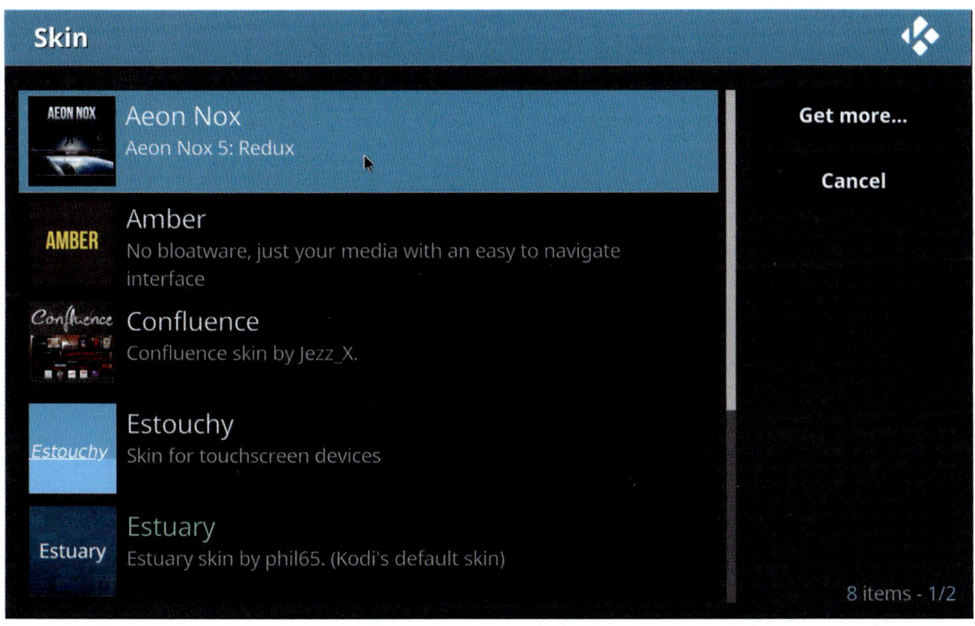

How to get subtitles in Kodi

If you're hard of hearing or just want to watch content silently, you can turn on subtitles on Kodi with this simple guide

If you're a regular Kodi user, you'll know just how great it is. It's extremely easy to customise, and, if you select the right combination of add-ons and skins, you can customise to exactly what you want. The only issue? As you'd expect from a free piece of open software, Kodi sometimes lacks polish, including simple features you usually take for granted, like subtitles. Just follow our step-by-step guide and you'll have subtitles for all your favourite TV shows and films forever.

1 Choose language and service

From the Kodi homescreen, go to Settings, Player and then select Language. Scroll down in the right-hand panel and you can set the language to English. Go to the next option, Default TV show service, and select it. Select Get more and then choose OpenSubtitles.org. Repeat for the Default Movie service.

2 Log in to service

To use OpenSubtitles.org you need to have a user account. Create one for free at opensubtitles.org. Click the Register button at the top, fill out the form and create a free user account. You have to verify your registration, so watch out for the incoming email, and then click the contained link and log in to the website. Back in Kodi, go to Add-ons, My Add-ons, All and find OpenSubtitles.org. Right-click the entry and select Settings. Now enter your username and password. Click OK.

3 Turn on subtitles

When you're watching a video, click on the subtitles icon in the bottom right. Then download (from OpenSubtitles.com). You'll see several different options, so pick the one with the best star rating to get the best subtitles.

Occasionally the text isn't exactly in sync with the onscreen dialogue. When this happens, click on the subtitles icon again and then select Subtitle Offset. With this, you can bring the text forward or backwards in time until it's lined up with what's happening onscreen.

It's worth noting that OpenSubtitles.org, as its name suggests is a free service. This means that there will be rare instances when the service doesn't work perfectly. When this happens, and you're desperate for subtitles, we suggest cycling through the other providers listed back in the home screen settings menu.

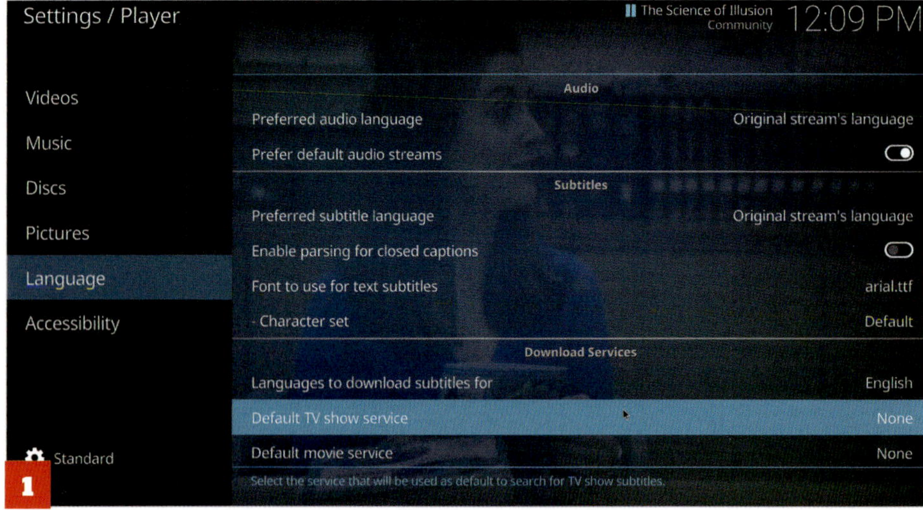

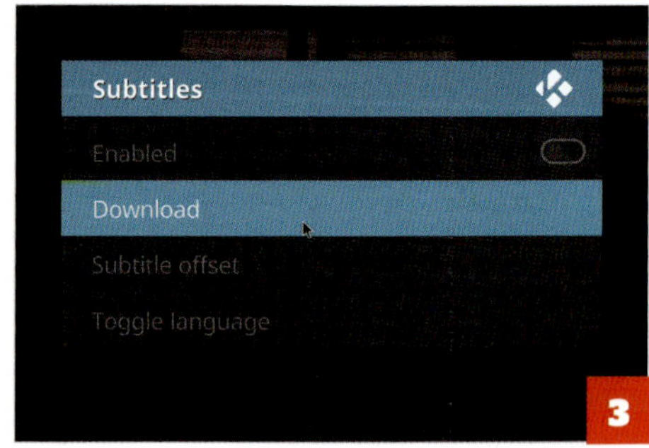

How to update to the latest build

Want the latest version of Kodi? Here's how to update to the latest build on all devices

Kodi releases regular updates for its system, but the exact steps you have to take depend on the type of device you're using. Unfortunately, Kodi doesn't have an automatic update feature built in, so you have to perform all updates manually, expect on Android. Here's how you manage each type of system.

PC and Mac

Both PC and Mac users can just download the latest version of Kodi from www.kodi.tv. Following our installation guide on pages 10 and 11 will work. Best of all, doing this will not affect or overwrite your library.

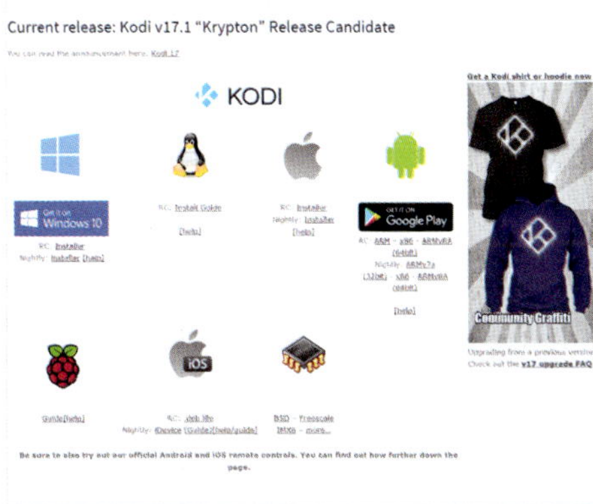

Android

Android users have it easy, as Kodi is available through the Play Store. This means that you can download the latest version straight from Google Play; if you have your phone set for automatic updates (the default option), Kodi will update automatically, too. All updates keep your existing settings and library preferences.

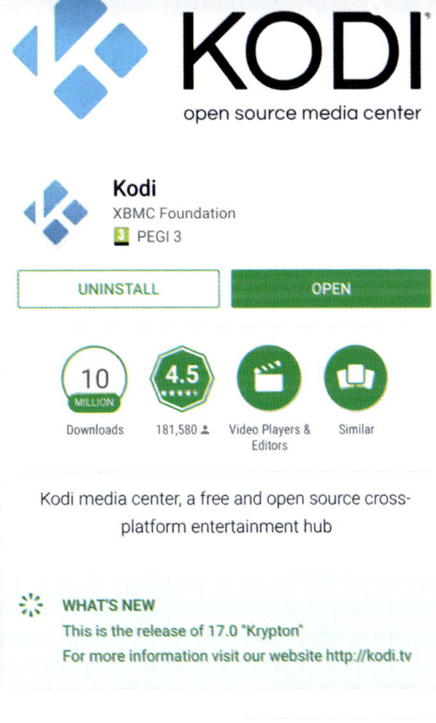

Amazon Fire TV Stick

Again, you're going to have to update manually for this one, following our in-depth installation guide on page 12. An update of this kind will overwrite the existing version of Kodi, but leave your settings in place.

Raspberry Pi

If you're using OSMC on the Raspberry Pi, then the update procedure is a little different. Do not follow our installation guide on page 14, as this will wipe your SD card and create a brand-new Kodi installation.

Instead, OSMC has a built-in update routine that will download the latest version of the OS and Kodi. This will run automatically and prompt you when to install. If you'd rather perform a manual update, you need to get a command line up. Type, 'sudo apt-get update', and then 'sudo-apt-get dist-upgrade'. This will download the latest version of the OS on demand, updating Kodi at the same time. This upgrade will leave all of your system settings alone, too.

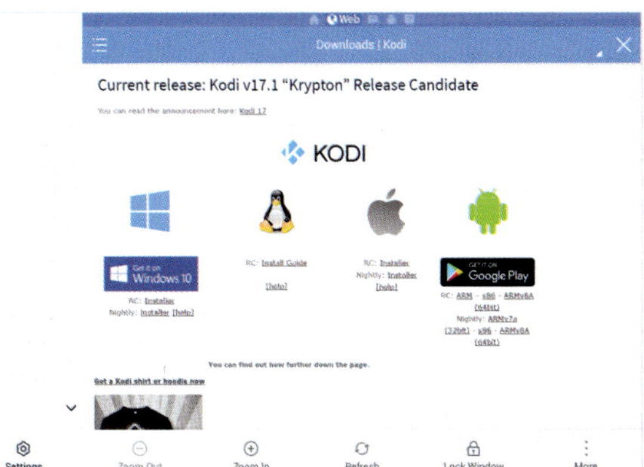

Best Kodi builds

Don't want to go to the hassle of installing your own add-ons? With a Kodi build, you get everything you need in one neat package

lthough Kodi is extremely flexible and lets you install loads of add-ons (see page 50), you may not want to go through the hassle of setting up everything manually. Fortunately, you don't have to, as you can also download pre-packaged Kodi builds. These take the core software, but bundle in all of the add-ons that you could want. It's important to remember, however, that Kodi builds aren't officially supported, so it may be better to download a clean version of Kodi and go from there. Some builds may let you view copyrighted material, so check before you stream and use them at your own risk to say on the right side of the law.

How to install a Kodi build

To install a Kodi build, you first need to have a regular installation of Kodi. The new build is then layered in on top of that, through the software's main menus. We'll show you the general steps to take, but you'll need to replace the source with the information that we've provided in our list of the best builds.

1 Add a source

Go to the Settings menu and select File Manager. Select Add source, then select <none>. Enter in the source web address name from our list of Best Kodi Builds and then click OK. Enter a name for the media source and click OK.

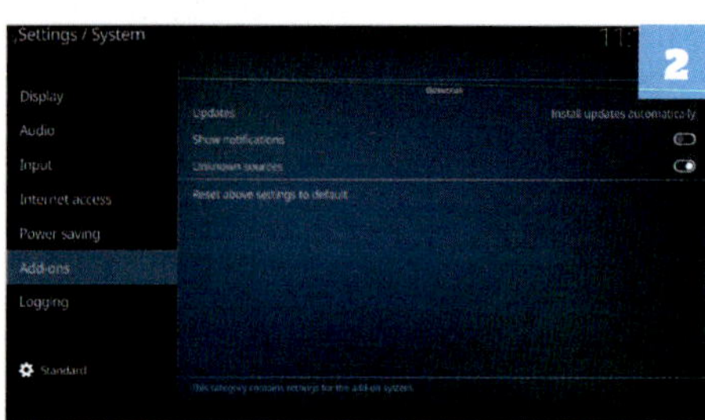

2 Enable unknown sources

To install most of the Kodi builds, you need to tell Kodi to allow installations from Unknown sources. Go to Settings, System and select Add-ons. Select the Unknown sources entry and toggle the option on.

3 Install from zip

You're now ready to install your chosen build. Go back to the Home screen and select Add-ons. In this menu, select the Package install icon (the box icon at the top left) and select Install from Zip file. Select the Source that you named in Step 1, and then select the Zip file you want (some repositories have multiple Zip files, but choose the one named after the build that you want and listed in our guide). Go back to the Home screen, and you'll get a pop-up telling you that your add-on has installed.

4 Configure your add-on

Go to Add-ons, My add-ons and select Program add-ons. Your new build should be be listed here. Select the wizard or option (our guide below tells you the exact option for each build), and follow the steps to complete the installation. If your build isn't listed, it's because it has to be installed in a slightly different way. Go to Add-ons, click the Package install icon and select install from Repository, then use the details in our listing to find the Repository name and installation option. Once you've done that, your build will be available in Add-ons as detailed above. Just follow the installation wizard through to get it working.

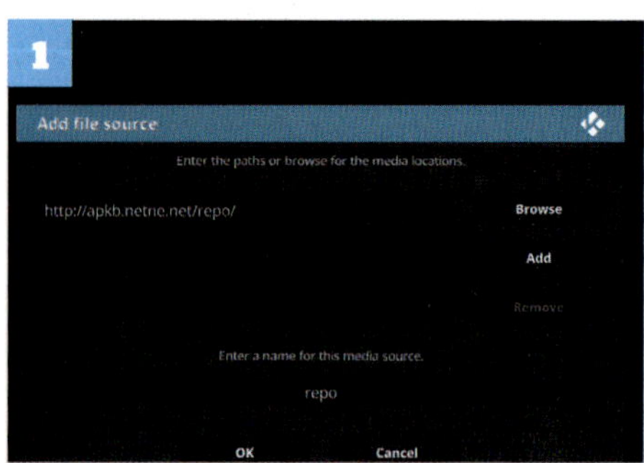

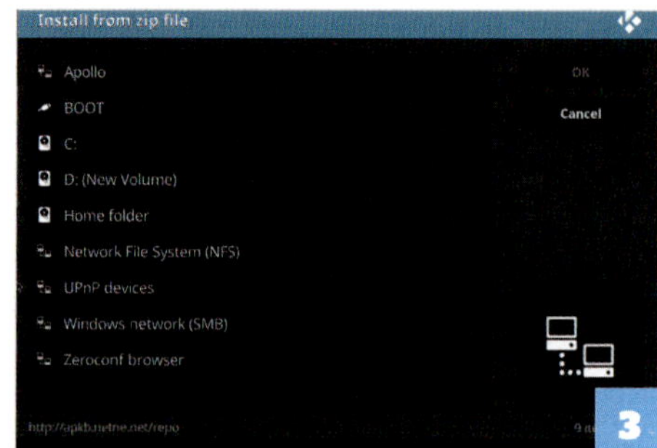

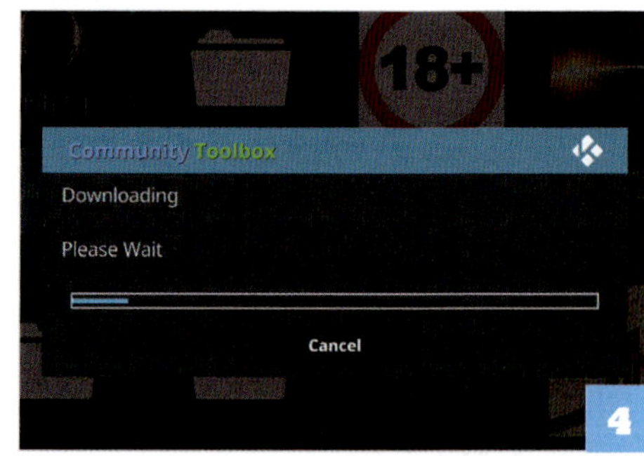

1 Tomb Raider

Source: http://echocoder.com/repo/
Zip: repository-echo.1.04.zip
Repository: Echo Repository, Program add-ons, Echo Wizard
Installation option: Echo Wizard, Community Builds, Tomb Raider, Tomb Raider Krypton Build

A neat, free build, Tomb Raider doesn't require a user account or any form of authentication, making it one of the best to get started with. A smart skin that makes navigation easy is just the starting point, but this build also comes with all of the most popular add-ons pre-packed, so you can get all of the great content that you want, too.

2 Apollo

Source: http://repo.ares-project.com/magic
Zip: script.areswizard.zip
Respository: Ares Project, Program add-ons, Ares Wizard
Installation option: Ares Wizard, Browse Builds, Apollo Build

Simply put, Apollo is one of the best builds you can get on Kodi right now. It uses a customised skin, so it looks great, but dig deeper and you'll find all the addons you could want – and a lot more. Despite its fully-featured nature, Apollo is actually very stable, so whether you're on a low-powered laptop or a Fire TV Stick, you shouldn't experience many crashes either. During the installation wizard, you'll be asked for a PIN; follow the on-screen instructions to get this and then choose Apollo AiOne (Krypton).

3 The Beast

Source: http://thebeast1.com/repo
Zip: plugin.video.beast.zip
Installation option: The Beast Wizard

Unlike other builds, The Beast isn't focused on one particular area of content, and instead, gives you a 360 choice of everything the family might want to watch. This makes it king of all content and is handy if you want to see everything that Kodi can offer, all without having to find every individual add-on that you might want. You need to create a user account, following the on-screen instructions to make this build work, though.

4 Hard Nox

Source: http://spinztvrepo.com/
Zip: repository.SpinzTv-0.1.1.zip
Repository: SpinzTV, Program add-ons, SpinzTV Wizard
Installation option: SpinzTV Wizard, Builds, SpinzTV Hard Nox Krypton, Standard Install

Using the Aeon Nox 5: Silvo Skin, Hard Nox is a fantastic-looking build. It's also only a few hundred megabytes in size, making it one of the most lightweight, too. This makes it ideal for lighter systems, such as a Fire TV Stick. Although it might not take long to download, Hard Nox comes pre-loaded with all of the add-ons that you're likely to want, to access tonnes of content.

5 Horizon

Source: http://echocoder.com/repo/
Zip: repository-echo.1.04.zip
Repository: Echo Repository, Program add-ons
Installation option: Echo Wizard, Community Builds, Samwich, Horizon Krypton, Download The Horizon Krypton Now

An excellent build for 2017, the makers of Horizon have picked one of the most intuitive skins, making it really easy to find the content that you want. And, what a choice of content, with all of the top plug-ins pre-installed and working, too. If you just want to dive in and get everything, Horizon is one of the freshest and best ways to get everything.

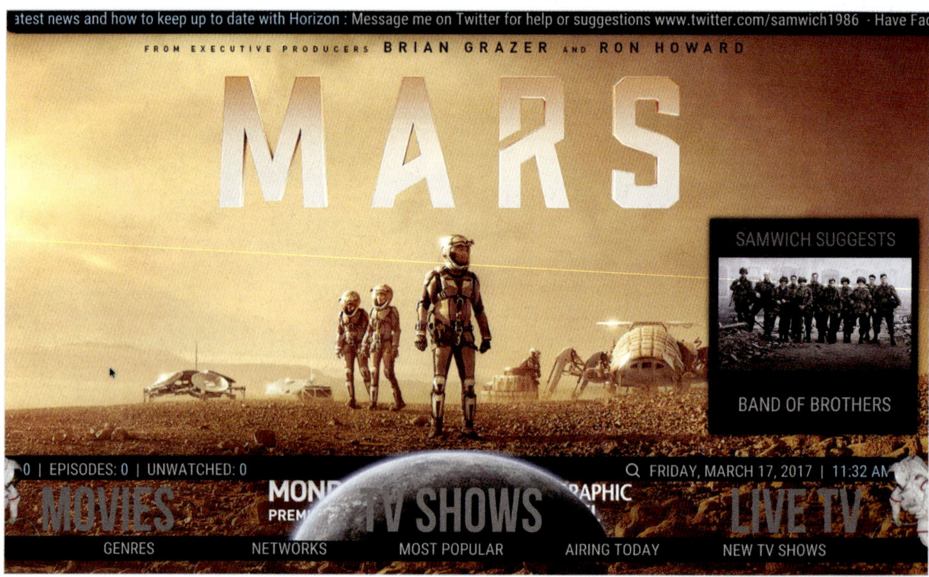

6 SpinzTV Premium Lite

Source: http://spinztvrepo.com
Zip: repository.SpinzTv-0.1.1.zip
Repository: SpinzTV, Program add-ons, SpinzTV Wizard
Installation option: SpinzTV, Builds, Spinz TV Premium Lite, Standard Install

As well as the excellent Hard Nox, SpinzTV has additional builds. Premium Lite is one of the best, with all of the add-ons that you could possibly want. However, it's also quite light-weight, making it a good choice for low-power systems, such as a Fire TV Stick. With an excellent and simple skin, SpinzTV Premium Light is exceptionally easy to navigate and works smoothly on all systems.

7 Ethereal

Source: http://echocoder.com/repo/
Zip: repository-echo.1.04.zip
Repository: Echo Repository, Program add-ons, Echo Wizard
Installation option: Echo Wizard, Community Builds, KodiApps, Ethereal 2.x, Download the Ethereal (Krypton) 2.x Now

Although Ethereal has all of the most popular add-ons, it also has its own unique Ethereal add-on, giving you access to even more content. Based around TV shows and sports, Ethereal has a lot of content that the entire family can watch. This makes it one of the best all-round builds for anyone with kids that cares more about TV that films. Note that some of the add-ons require simple activation to work, following the on-screen information.

8 Duggz Build

Source: http://duggzbuilds.uk/repo/
Zip: plugin.video.DuggzBuilds.zip
Respository: N/A
Installation option: Duggz Builds Wizard, Duggz Pro Prem & Free Krypton

Duggz Build is one of the oldest builds available, but it's still one of the best. It has all of the main add-ons that you could want, with this version focussing on sports. With a slick new skin, finding the content that you want to watch is incredibly easy. As the add-on has been around for so long, you have confidence that will be updated and kept fresh, too.

9 JayHawk

Source: http://echocoder.com/repo/
Zip: repository-echo.1.04.zip
Repository: Echo Repository, Program add-ons, Echo Wizard
Installation option: Echo Wizard, Community Builds, JayHawk Media, Jayhawk4-k17v1.02 For Kodi 17 Krypton, Download The Jayhawk 4-k17V1.0.2 For Kodi 17 Krypton Now

JayHawk is a new build for 2017, from a new developer. It looks set to be one of the best, too. It's very lightweight, so should run well on practically every device from a Raspberry Pi 3 to a Fire TV Stick and beyond. It's also packed with content, with practically every single add-on that you could want pre-installed and working, ready to go, and its simple and straightforward skin makes finding the content you want easy.

How to get the best Kodi skins

There's no need to stick with the basic Kodi interface, as skins let you completely change the way the media player looks and feels

Simply put, Kodi skins change the entire look and feel of the media player, completely replacing the standard interface. Best of all, skins are completely free, so you experiment with different ones until you find the one that like the best. We've picked our favourite skins on this page, with all of them available in the official Kodi repository. This makes them super easy to install.

Just go to Settings, Interface and click the Skin option (the default setting is Estuary). Click the Get more button and you'll see a big list of all of the available skins. Just select the one you want and Kodi will download it. You now need to go back to the Skin option and select your downloaded Skin from the main list.

BEST SKINS

Xperience1080

Kodi is great in its original form, but Xperience1080 offers a slightly better user experience. Xperience1080 is panel-based so it's very easy to understand and navigate, and if you've got an Xbox One, you'll find it looks very familiar. Using the home screen is extremely intuitive, and the clever design continues throughout the theme.

Aeon Nox

If you like Confluence – the default skin for older Kodi versions – then chances are you'll like Aeon Nox. Although it looks stylish, it's not too much of a burden on your system. The result? It looks good, but it also runs smoothly on even the smallest devices, such as the Amazon Fire TV Stick.

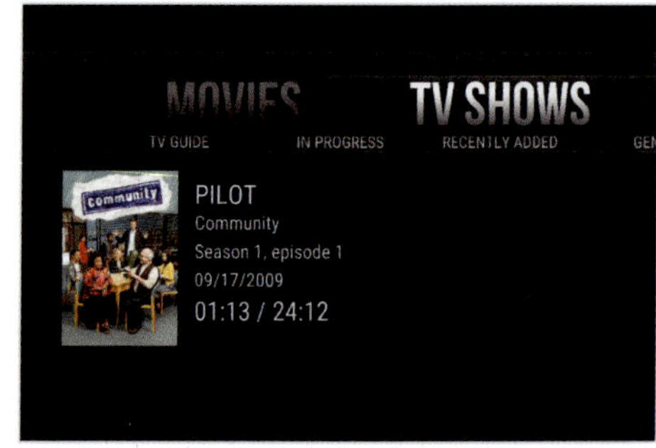

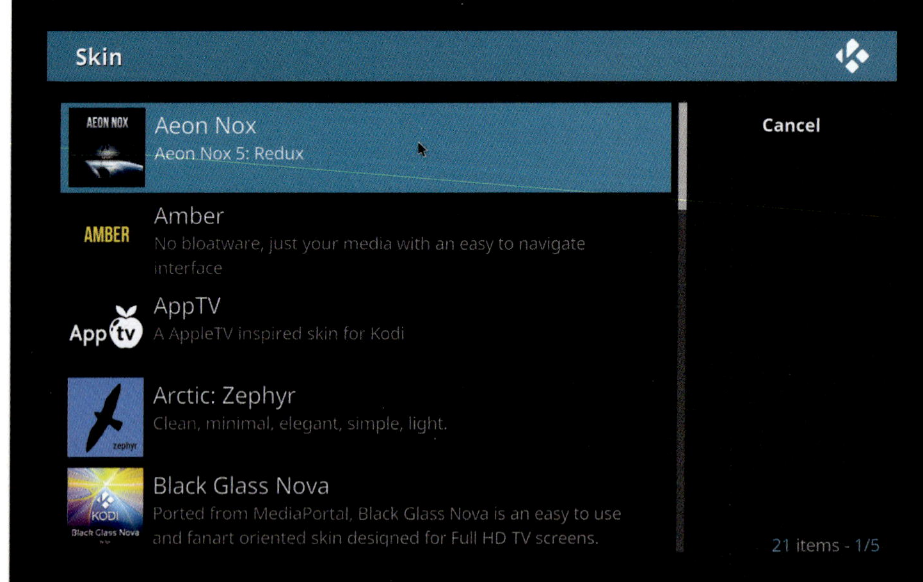

Amber

Amber might not look like the most exciting Kodi skin, but it offers and light, easy to read interface that won't bog down your device. Text is sharp and clear while navigating menus is rapid - even on slower devices. It's not the most sophisticated skin we've seen, but it does the job perfectly.

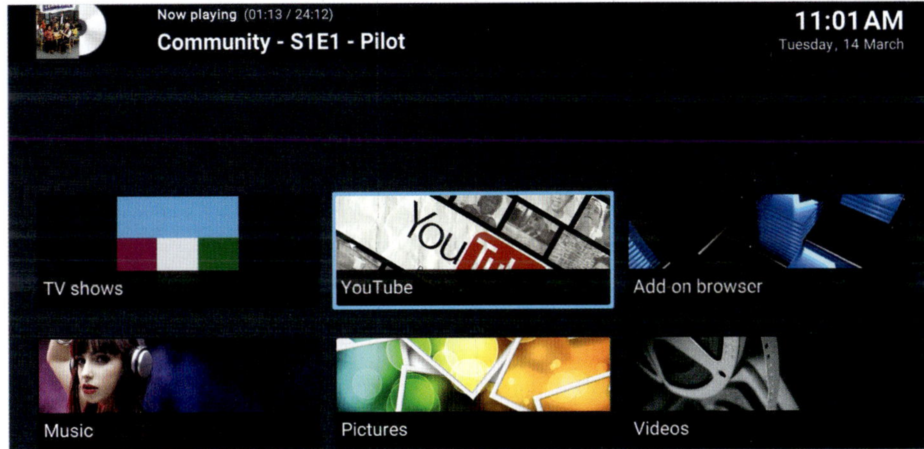

Metropolis

Metropolis is designed to blend retro and the future, a bit like a 1930s sci-fi film. It does a brilliant job, and the settings screen with its art-deco style icons is absolutely beautiful. If you want a Kodi skin that really looks different, then Metropolis is the one that we recommend installing.

Titan

Another skin designed to be simple and effective, Titan does exactly that. It's pretty, but makes it easy for you to pick your next film or TV show. But the best thing about Titan? Its simple user interface is ideal for smaller devices.

Confluence

Confluence was the default skin for Kodi, until the most recent version, with good reason. It's clear, intuitive and stylish, and is probably one of the best Kodi skins available. Downloading new and different-looking skins is easy, but if you'd rather get down to watching films and TV shows, there's no harm in staying with Kodi's original skin, particularly if this is what you're used to.

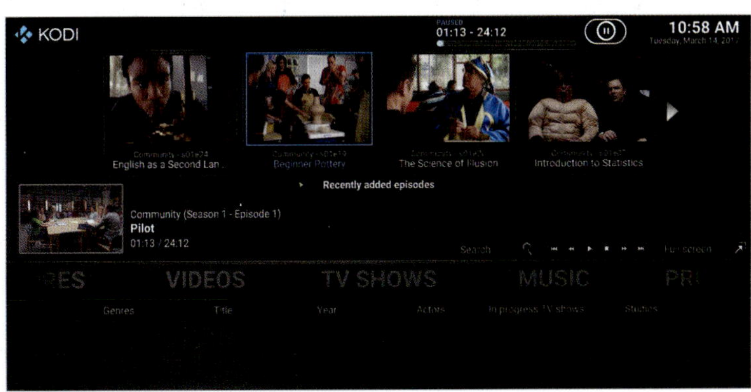

How to use a VPN with Kodi

A VPN can keep your Kodi use anonymous, protecting you from any snooping. Here's how to set one up

When you use Kodi (or any network connected device), your ISP can see exactly what you're looking at and what device you're using. If you'd rather keep your browsing habits secure and safe, you need to use a Virtual Private Network (VPN) instead. A VPN can also help you unlock new content, by masking your location.

How does a VPN work?

Normally, when you connect to a service, your internet traffic passes through your ISP's network and out onto the web. The device that you connect to can then see your IP address, so it knows both who you are and which country you're located in. With a VPN, things are different. Your traffic is encrypted so that your ISP can't see what you're looking at. Traffic is encrypted until it hits a VPN endpoint. Thanks to this, any service you connect to can't see your IP address, but only the address of the VPN endpoint. Effectively, by using a VPN, you stop both ISPs and websites/web services from being to tell who you are, keeping your Kodi usage a complete secret.

What other benefits are there?

As well as hiding who you are and what you're looking at, using a VPN can have other advantages. If the endpoint is in a different country, such as the US, it looks as though you're located in the same place. This can unlock extra content, such as US Netflix (see page 76).

How can I use a VPN?

To use a VPN, you have to first sign up for a service (we list our favourite ones over the next few pages). You also need a device that you can install a VPN client on, including Windows, Mac and Android. Unfortunately, other devices, such as the Amazon Fire TV stick don't have easily-installable clients. In this case, you need a router running a VPN, and you then connect your Kodi box to that network (see page 78 for more details).

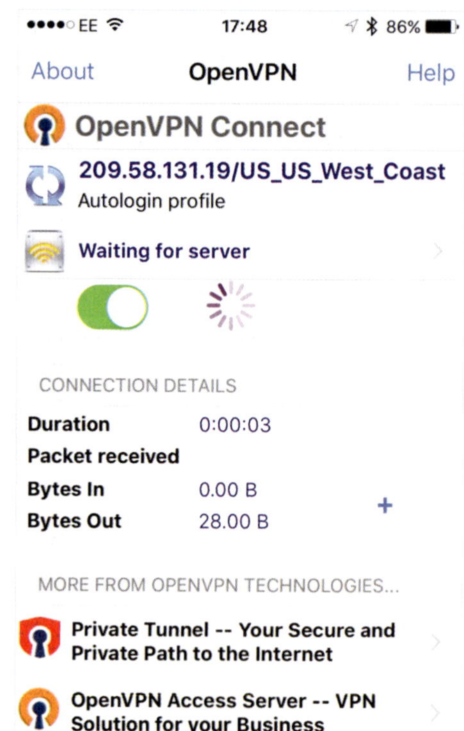

Best VPNs for Kodi

Looking for a VPN? Here are the best ones that we've used with Kodi

There's a massive range of VPNs available, with prices varying hugely. In truth, it depends on exactly what you want to do, as to which product is best for you. Most services have a free trial, so you can download and give the service a go before you commit to paying for it. This way, you get to see how good a VPN is before you start paying for it. It's also worth paying attention to see if a service covers US Netflix, too (our round-up tells you).

Our list covers a large range of VPNs, including one that's completely free. We only recommend using a free service for light use. This is because these VPNs are throttled, reducing the speed of connection that you get. In turn, this can have a massive impact on performance, resulting in low-quality or jerky video streams. When you pay for a service, you get much faster throughputs.

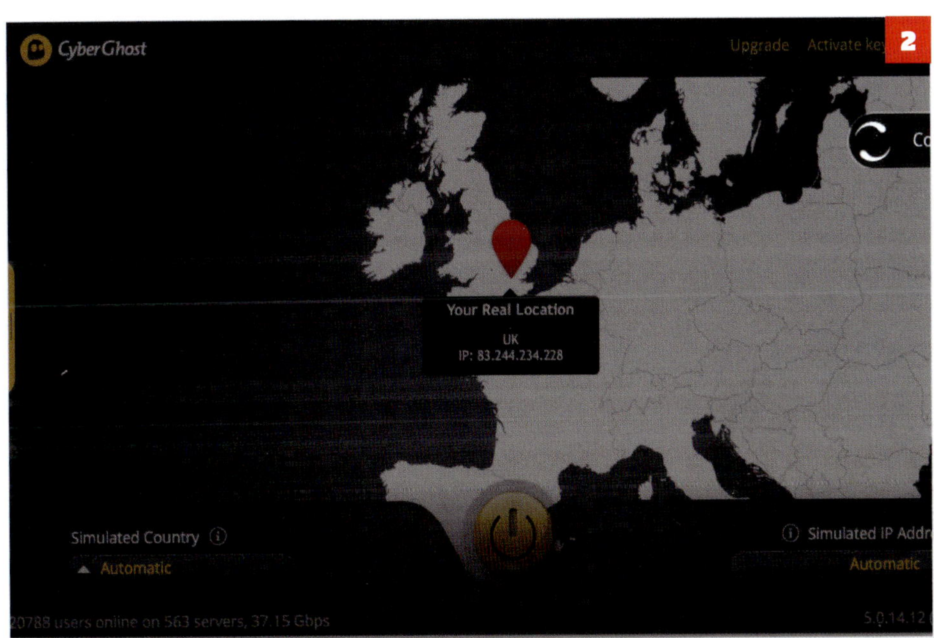

1 Buffered VPN ($8.25/month)
From buffered.com

If you want something quick and easy to use, and you're not worried about paying a little more, than the Buffered VPN represents a great choice. It's almost always fast, extremely easy to use, and it works with all the streaming services you'd expect, and it's still one of the best chances you have at unblocking geolocked content such as US Netflix. You can sign up to Buffered for $8.25 per month for a year, but if you're not happy, Buffered also offers a 30-day money-back guarantee.

2 CyberGhost VPN (from Free)
From www.cyberghostvpn.com

CyberGhost is a really well-known VPN, and after using it for just a short time it's easy to see why. Simply put, CyberGhost is one of the easiest VPNs to use, and lets you start a VPN and browser session with just one click. Just like other VPNs such as ExpressVPN and IPVanish, CyberGhost doesn't store details of your connection activity either. Oh, and one more thing, CyberGhost can be used for free. Sure, you won't always have immediate access to servers like a paying customer, but it's a great way to try out the service to see if you want a VPN. For better performance and a faster connection, you can currently get CyberGhost on a £4 PAYG basis.

3 ExpressVPN ($8/month)
From www.expressvpn.com

Although ExpressVPN isn't as well known in the Kodi community, it's still one of the best VPNs you can use for Kodi. ExpressVPN doesn't store any activity logs, so your privacy is maintained, and it's also historically been one of the best VPNs for watching US Netflix in the UK, too. But the best thing? ExpressVPN comes with a great support network, and if you're unsure about or satisfied with the service, you can take advantage of its 30-day money-back guarantee. After that, ExpressVPN will cost you $8 per month for a 12-month contract.

4 NordVPN ($3/month)
From www.nordvpn.com

NordVPN is currently one of the most powerful VPNs services you can get. Thanks to 695 worldwide server locations in 54 different countries, NordVPN has great coverage, so you can use it to connect from and to pretty much anywhere. What's more, NordVPN also has easy-to-use software, and as with other VPNs, it doesn't log or store your connection details. Finally, just like the other VPNs mentioned here, NordVPN uses a killswitch that shuts down your entire connection if your VPN ever goes down. That means there's no way your actual IP information can get leaked. At the time of writing, you can get NordVPN for just $3 per month.

5 IPVanish ($6/month)
From www.ipvanish.com

There are several Kodi VPNs around right now, but IPVanish is certainly one of the most popular among the Kodi community – and that's partly because of how much freedom it allows. IPVanish allows for the user of torrent services, and it also stops your browsing history being stored.

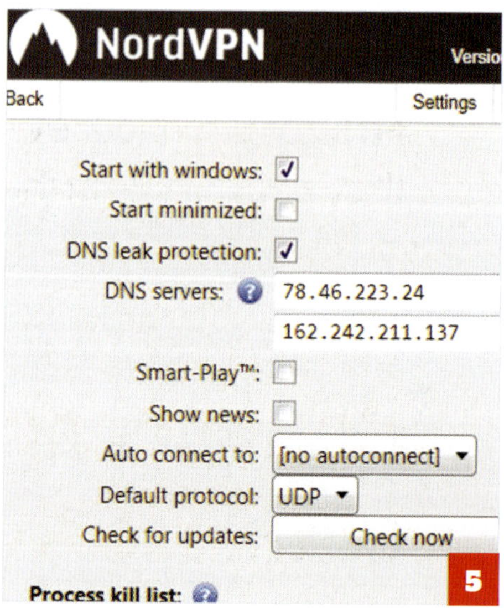

How to stop Kodi buffering

Is video constantly pausing and not playing smoothly? Here's how to fix the issues for good

Kodi is probably the ultimate streaming solution, but like any service that uses the internet, you're at the mercy of your broadband or data connection. When you're connected to a high-speed internet connection, Kodi can look lush, but when your connection isn't the best, things can get a little ropey.

If you've got a poor connection or there's something wrong with Kodi, you'll end up staring at a screen with a rotating logo. If this happens every few seconds, it's annoying and means that you can't enjoy any streamed video. We're here to help with a few ideas to make Kodi more reliable.

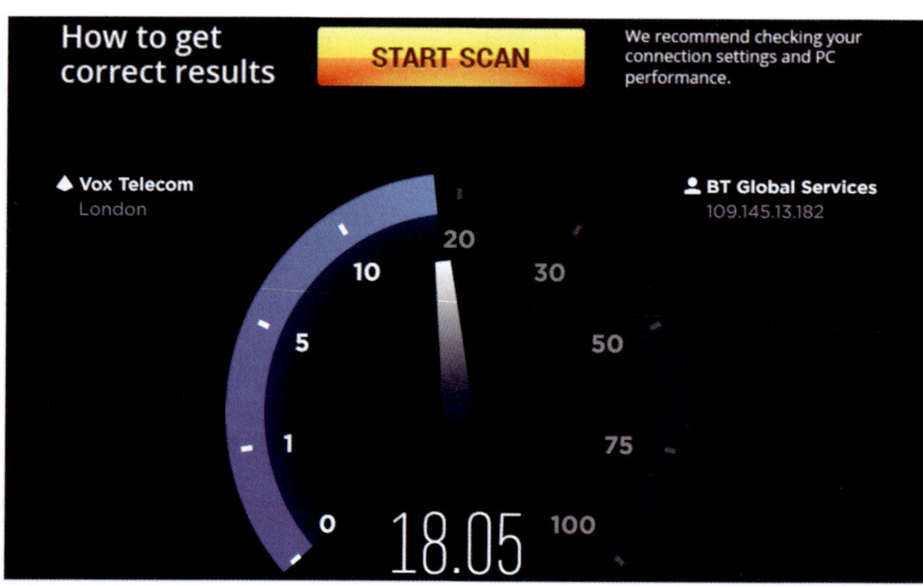

To start with, we'll show you how to check your internet connection to make sure there's nothing wrong there. Once you've done that, the solution gets a bit more technical, but we'll talk you through what you have to do.

1 Test your internet connection

Before you even delve into the software, your first start should be testing your internet connection. Generally, HD content will need a connection speed of at least 10Mbits/sec, so go to speedtest.net to see exactly what you're working with.

2 Fix internal probelms

If your speed is under 10Mbits/sec, check to make sure you're not too far from your router. Also make sure that no other devices are streaming, downloading or

doing any other larger tasks that could suck up your bandwidth. If there are other active devices, turn them off.

3 Fix the Kodi cache

If you find your stream is still lagging, it's worth effectively opening up the bonnet, and tweaking a few of Kodi's cache settings. Cache is used to buffer content in local storage. That way, if your internet connection slows down, Kodi can continue playing from the cache temporarily. The bigger the cache the better, as more video can be buffered. The only issue is that cache takes up memory, and since Kodi is designed to run on something as small as a Google Chromecast, it doesn't use much of it. However, there's a way to increase the amount of cache Kodi uses, and that's done via the advancedsettings XML file. Tweaking Kodi's buffering systems requires some fairly basic coding, but to make things easier, we've written it out for you below:

```
<advancedsettings>

<network>

<buffermode> 1 </buffermode>

<readbufferfactor> 1.5 </
readbufferfactor>

<cachemembuffersize>
104857600 </
cachemembuffersize>

</network>

</advancedsettings>
```

Enter the above, exactly as it appears, into a notepad file, and then make sure it's saved exactly as advancedsettings.xml - make sure Windows doesn't chage the file extension. Once that's done, you'll need to drop the file into your Kodi user data folder, but the location varies depending on the version of Kodi you're running.

Android
Android/data/org.xbmc.kodi/files/.kodi/userdata/

Linux/Raspberry Pi
~/.kodi/userdata/

Mac
/Users/<your_user_name>/Library/Application Support/Kodi/userdata/

Windows
%APPDATA%\kodi\userdata (Enter this into an Explorer window's address bar)

If you've done all of the above, you should find Kodi is running smoother and faster than ever before.

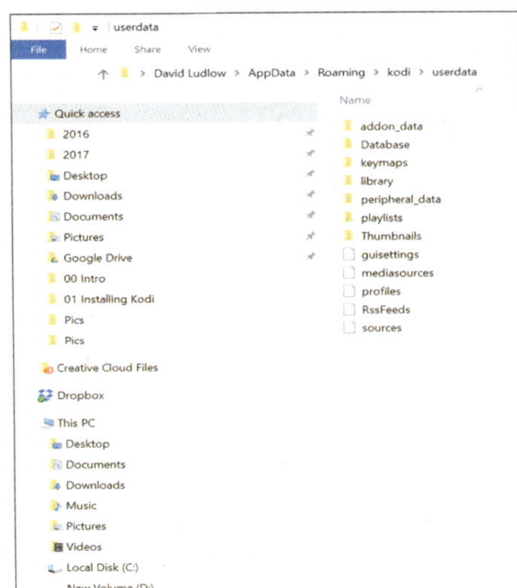

Chapter
4

Kodi add-ons

IN THIS SECTION

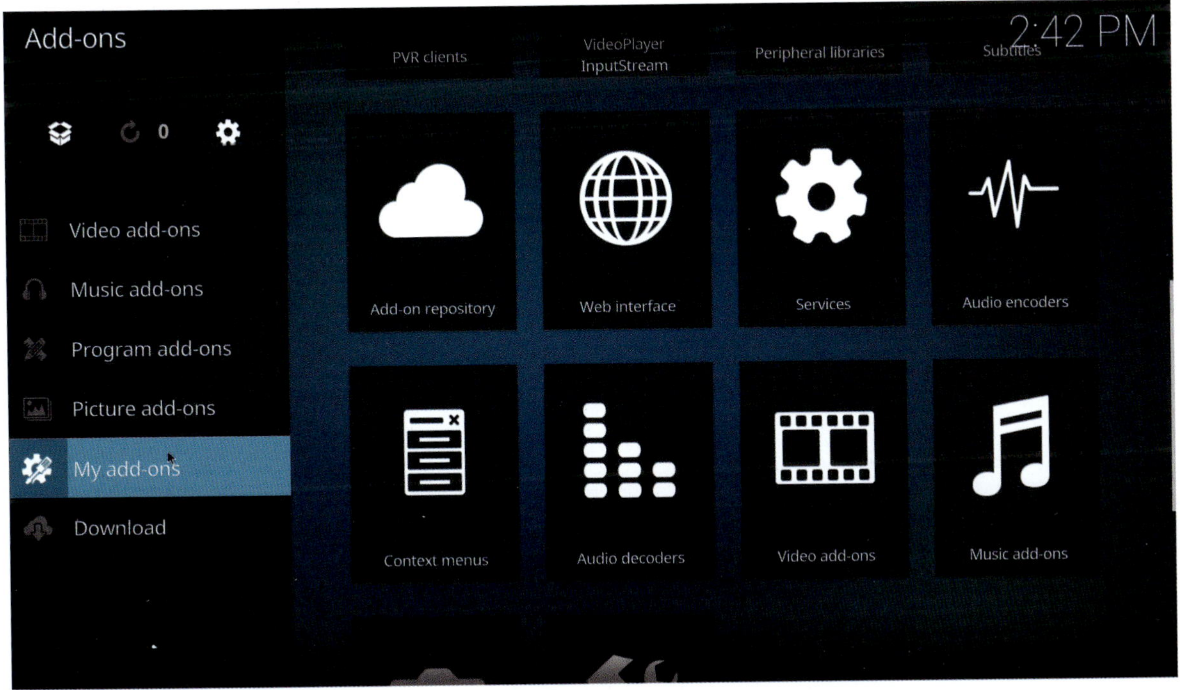

How to manage official Kodi add-ons

You can make your Kodi box do more with the brilliant, free, official add-ons. We'll show you how to install and manage them

While there are loads of third-party Kodi add-ons available that give you access to lots of content, you shouldn't ignore the best built-in ones. Available from the official Kodi repository, these add-ons are guaranteed to only access legal content and be free of malware.

There's a huge range on offer and, as they're available from inside Kodi, they're incredibly easy to install and manage. We'll take you through everything that you need to know, and then show you our favourite add-ons.

1 Find add-ons

The easiest way to install an add-on is to go to the Add-ons section and scroll down to Download. Once you've selected this, you get a list of add-on categories to choose from (see following pages for more information). Browse through the categories, and you can select individual add-ons to see more information about them.

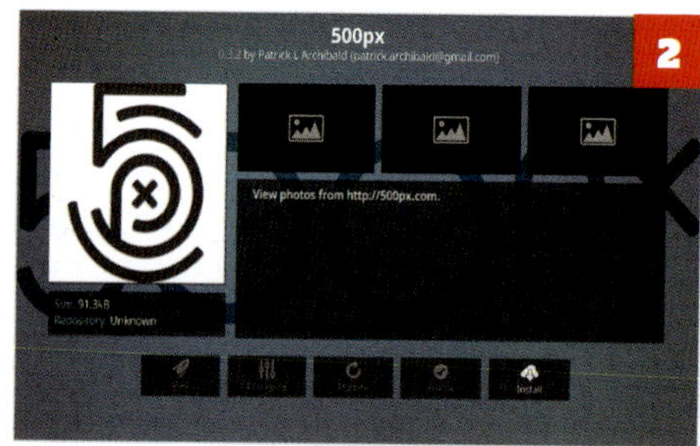

2 Install add-ons

Select an add-on, and you'll be taken to the information screen. Select the Install button, and the add-on will be automatically downloaded and installed to your Kodi box. You'll be given a notification when the add-on is ready for use.

3 Run an add-on

Once an add-on has been installed, you can find most of them in the Add-ons section of the main menu. Kodi splits add-ons out into categories: Photos, Videos, Music and Program. Select these sub-categories to find your installed add-on.

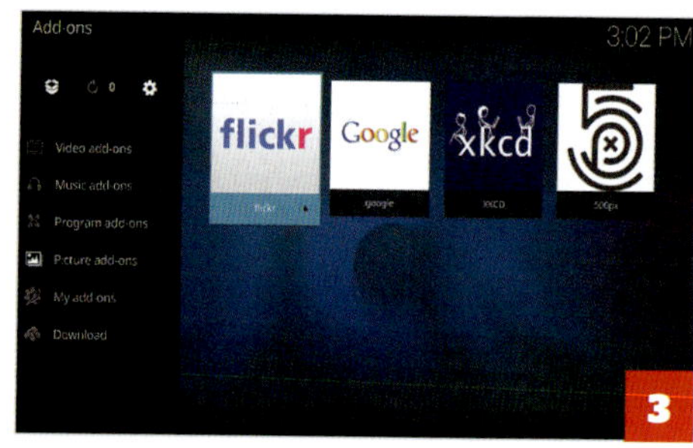

Note that not all add-ons appear here; Skins, screensavers and other customisation options can be accessed through settings.

4 Manage or uninstall add-ons

To find which add-ons you have installed go to Add-ons and select My add-ons. You can now browse through the categories of add-ons: those with a tick next to them are installed, those with a cross are not. Select an installed add-on, and you can use the Configure button to change settings and customise it. Use the Uninstall option to remove an add-on.

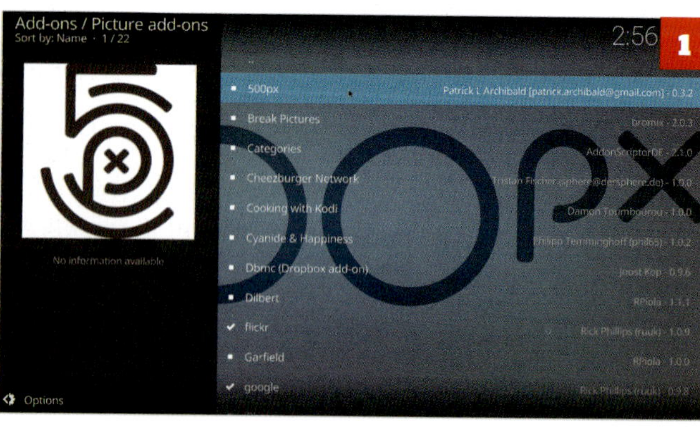

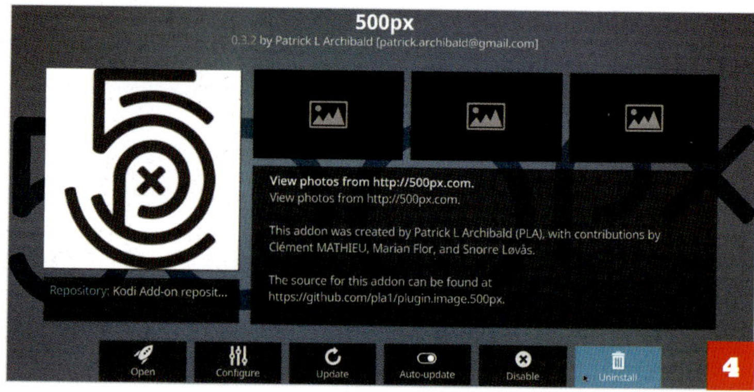

The best official Kodi add-ons

We've trawled through all of the major add-ons, so that you don't have to

There are lots and lots of official Kodi add-ons. On the previous page we described how to install and manage them, but here we'll explain what each add-on section is for. Where appropriate, we've also listed the best add-ons that you should install.

Information providers

This section provides add-ons that give you more information on media, such as details on an artist or album. By default, all of these add-ons are installed and are running, so there's little need to do anything here.

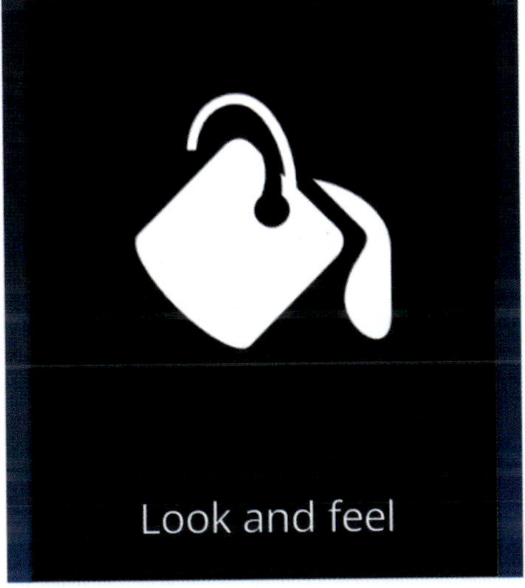

Look and feel

This section lets you download new interface sounds, screensavers and icon artwork. These options can all be managed in an easier way through the Settings app. We show you how to change Skins on page 42 of this book.

Game add-ons

This section lets you down new controller layouts for gamepads, ranging from the original NES to the PlayStation. Rather than managing the settings here, go to Settings, System Settings and select Configure attached controllers. You'll need to have a game controller plugged into Kodi to use it to control menus and playback.

Weather

Kodi has a built-in weather section, available from the main menu. However, you need a weather app to make the most of it. You can download one from the Weather section. We recommend OpenWeatherMap Extended. Select this add-on and choose Install, then choose Configure and you get set up to five weather locations. View current and upcoming weather using the Weather option in the main menu.

Subtitles

From this section, you can download and manage all of the subtitle add-ons. OpenSubtitles.org is the best option, but you're better off following our guide on how to download and configure it (see page 36 for more details).

Lyrics

Want to sing along with your favourite tracks? Select Lyrics and install the CU LRC Lyrics add-on (the only one available). When you play a track, this add-on will pop-up a box with matching lyrics. It's pretty accurate, too, picking up most of the popular tracks we played; you may have more trouble with slightly more obscure artists.

Web interface

This section lets you download add-ons to let you remote control Kodi through a web browser. Ignore this section, as the best thing to do, is follow our guide on page 22, as the web interface needs a little configuration and explanation.

Services

The Services section contains lots of neat little add-ons for display information or integrating with other services. For football fans, the Fussball Ticker will show live game stats in a pop-up window. Get Last.fm if you already use the service on other devices. Unpause Jumpback is a handy add-on that lets you jump back a set number of seconds when coming out of pause, so that you can catch up on the action and get back into a film.

Video add-ons

With the Video add-ons section, you get some of the best Kodi upgrades. This section has a mix of free content and content that you need an account or activation code for. There's a lot in there, so it's worth spending some time finding the content that you want.
It's worth installing iPlayer WWW, so you can get catch-up content. YouTube is a great choice, too. We're fans of ComingSoon, so that we can keep up-to-date with the latest film trailers.

Music add-ons

There are tonnes of free music services to add using the Music add-ons section. Grab the Apple iTunes Podcasts if you listen to a lot of these. If you want the latest movie news and reviews, Kermode and Mayo's Film Review is a great choice. There's support for the Tidal streaming service, too, but no official Spotify support. Radio is a great add-on if you want thousands of radio stations to listen to.

Picture add-ons

If anything, the Picture add-ons section is a little disappointing, and there aren't quite the same quality range of services as for video and audio. Flickr support, for example, is tricky to tie into your user account, so it acts more like a search engine for the site. The Maps Browser option to show you where you images were taken on a map is a useful add-on (see page 30 for more information).

Program add-ons

Program add-ons gives you some additional standalone features that you can launch directly from Kodi. There's a big range on offer, with some pre-installed, such as the tool to display album artwork for music tracks. Out of everything, we like Dbmc, the Dropbox add-on; Facebook Media for looking at the social network's images; Match center for current football scores and tables; and Plex, so you can connect to a Plex server for streaming movies, audio and TV.

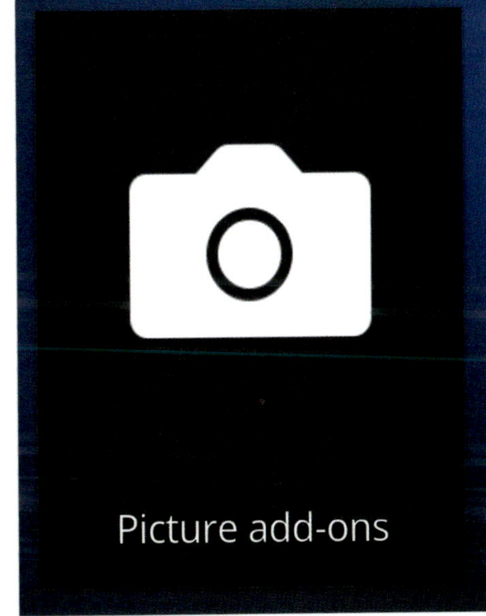

How to install other add-ons

There are lots of unofficial Kodi add-ons, giving you access to a wide-range of services. Here's how to install them

As it's completely open-source, anyone is free to write their own add-ons for Kodi. These fall outside of the officially supported add-ons, and give you access to a wide-range of content. We have to say that some of the content available may be copyrighted, so check before you start to stream anything. As we pointed out on page 6, Kodi add-ons may not strictly be illegal (for now), but morally you may access content that you shouldn't.

You also take a risk with any third-party add-on. All of the main add-ons have been checked to ensure that they're free of malware and work properly. Third-party add-ons do not carry that claim, so may cause problems. Again, install at your own risk.

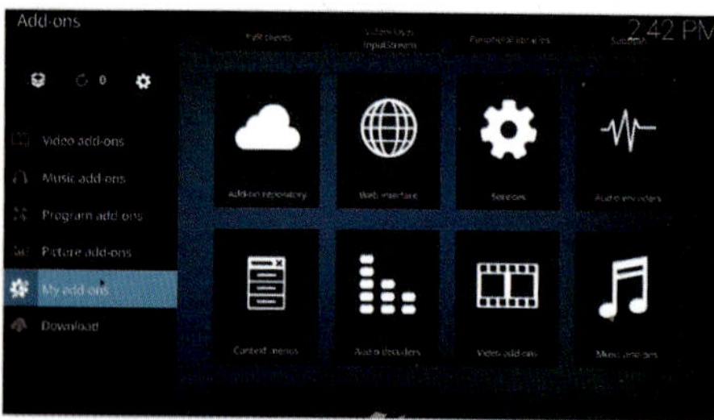

These add-ons will give you access to tonnes of content streamed live from the internet. To install them, you'll need to follow our guide, and you'll also need to note down both the repository source and the correct installation option from our bess add-on listing. This is because many repositories contain multiple add-ons.

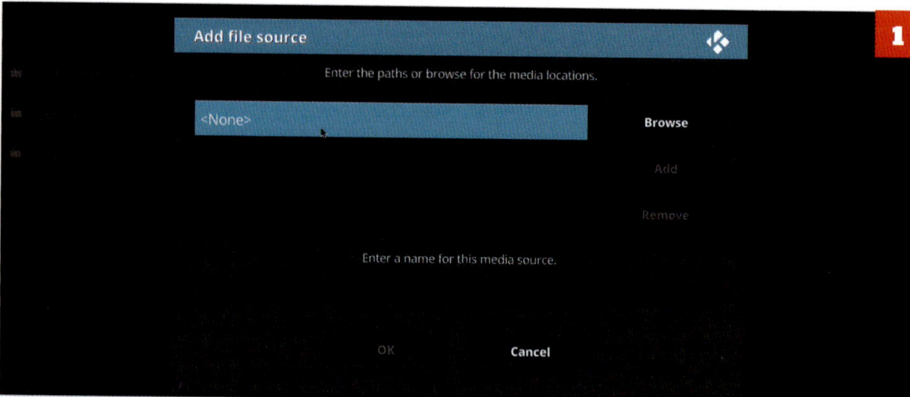

These add-ons change quickly and streams can break, so you may need to try a few before you get the content that you want.

1 Add a Source

First, you need to add the add-ons repository into Kodi, so that it knows where to download content from. To do this, go to Settings, File manager and select Add source. Enter the source address (effectively, a web address), exactly as it appears, as listed in our guide. Next, give it a name (we suggest using the name of the add-on for simplicity).

2 Allow unknown sources

For protection, Kodi will not let you install files from just anywhere. To override this protection, you need to go to Settings, System Settings. Select Add-ons and then turn on the Unknown sources option listed under General. You can now install add-ons from anywhere.

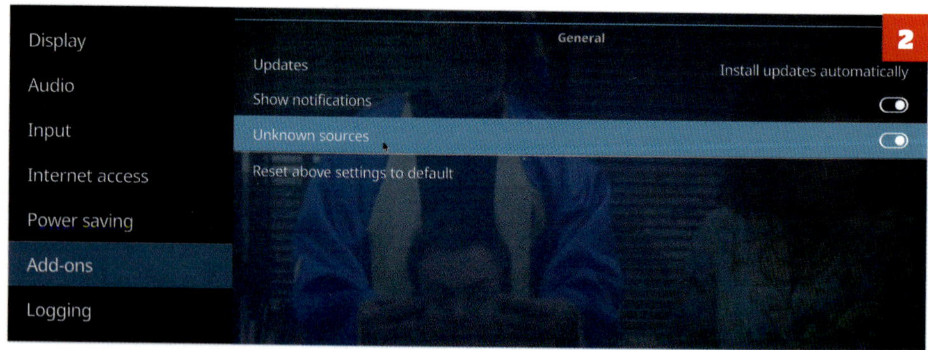

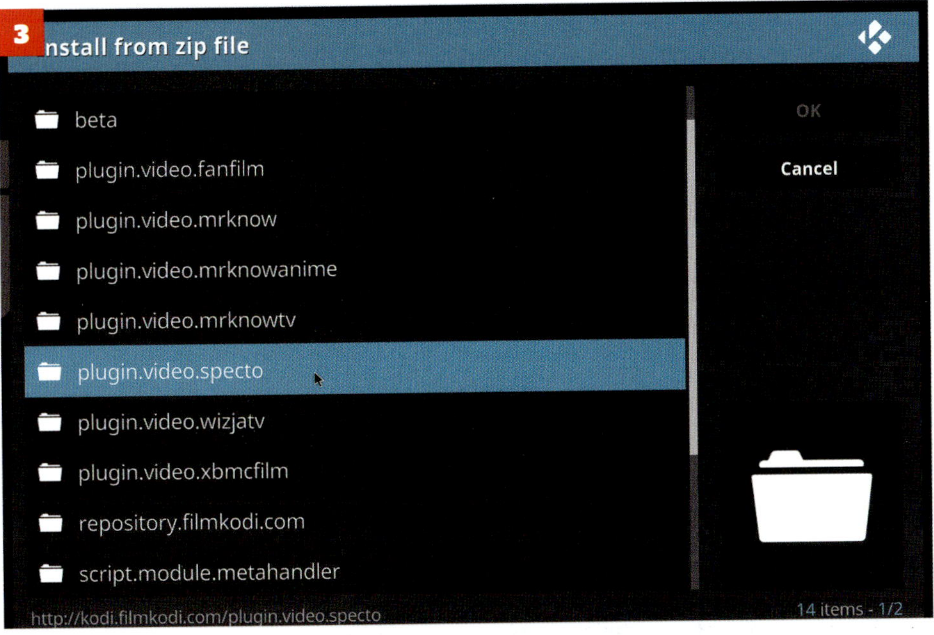

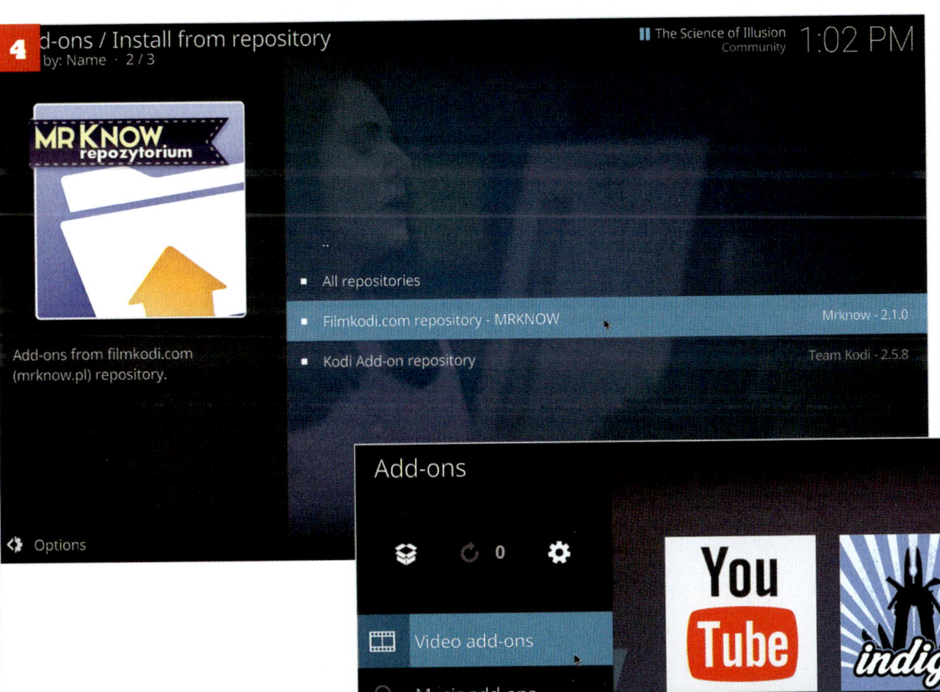

3 Install the add-on

You're now ready to install your chosen build. Go back to the Home screen and select Add-ons. In this menu, select the Package install icon (the box icon at the top left) and select Install from Zip file. Select the Source that you named in Step 1, and then select the Zip file you want (some sources have multiple Zip files, but choose the one named in our listing). Go back to the Home screen, and you'll get a pop-up telling you that your add-on has installed. This usually just installs a new Repository, so you then need to download the actual add-on.

4 Install from repository

Go back to the Home screen and select Add-ons. In this menu, select the Package install icon (the box icon at the top left) and select Install from Repository. Our listings show you the path you need to take to select the right add-on. Once you've done that, select the Install button. The add-on will be downloaded to your Kodi box and will be ready to run.

5 Run your add-on

Once you've installed an add-on, you can find it my going to Add-ons in the main menu. In the sub menu, you can browse add-ons by their sub-category: Video, Pictures, Music and Program. Just select the add-on you want from the right sub-category and run it. From the add-on, select the content you want to view.

Best Kodi add-ons

These are the best Kodi add-ons currently available and will give you access to loads of new content

1 Specto

Source: http://kodi.filmkodi.com
Zip: repository.filmkodi.com, repository.filmkodi.com-x.x.x.zip
Repository: Filmkodi.com repository – MRKNOW, Video add-ons, Specto - ...Fork

Simply put, Specto is the Genesis add-on resurrected and updated for 2017, complete with working links. Like Genesis before it, Specto now has one the most well-rounded collection of links so that you can stream TV shows and films suitable for all the family. So, want to download one of the most highly regarded Kodi add-ons in a new, refreshed form? Grab a copy of Specto today, then.

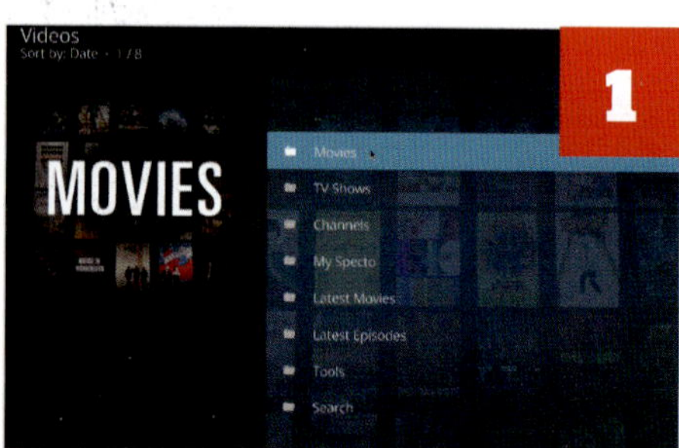

2 1Channel Primewire

Source: http://fusion.tvaddons.ag
Zip: kodi-repos, english, repository.tknorris.release-x.x.x.zip
Repository: tknorris release repository, Video add-ons, 1Channel

The 1Channel Primewire extension is one of the most popular Kodi add-ons in 2017, and that's because it features pretty much everything. In fact, if you're not

too bothered about customising Kodi, 1Channel Primewire could, alongside Exodus or Specto, be one of the only addons you'll need.

3 UK Turk's Playlists

Source: http://kodi.metalkettle.co
Zip: repository.metalkettle-x.x.x.zip
Repository: MetalKettles Addon Repository, Video add-ons, UK Turk Playlists

What makes UK Turk's Playlists one of the best add-ons you can get right now? Simply put, it offers a variety of content, from cartoons and documentaries to comedy and fitness shows. If that sounds like the sort of thing you'd be interested in, install it now.

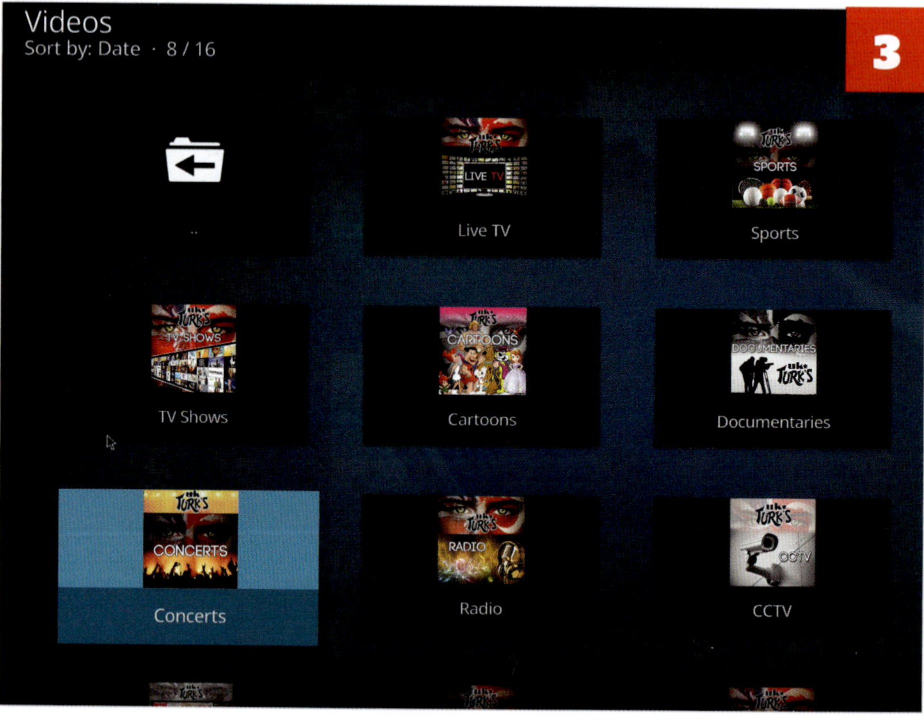

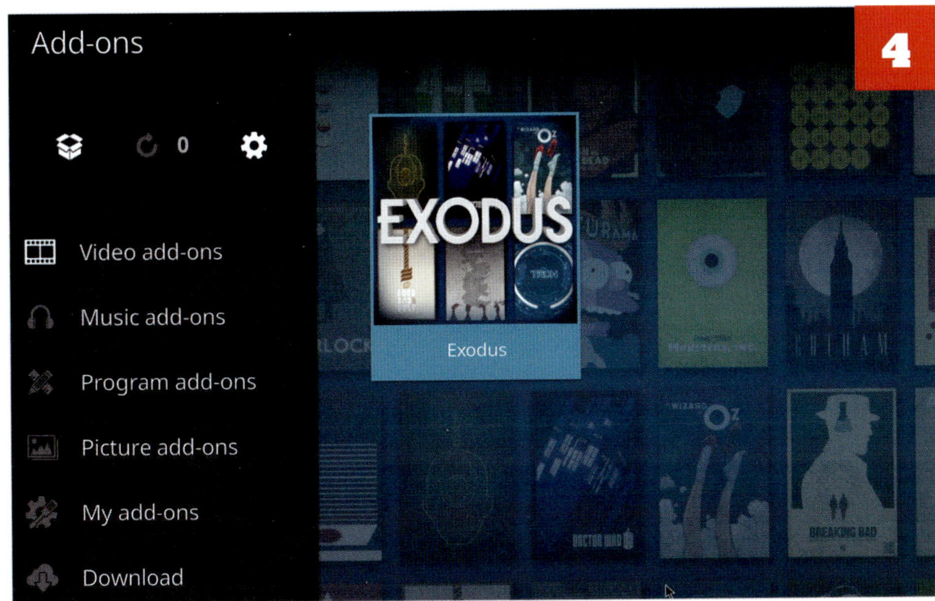

4 Exodus

Source: http://fusion.tvaddons.ag
Zip: kodi-repos, english, repo. exodus.x.x.x.x.zip
Repository: Exodus repository, Video add-ons, Exodus

Genesis used to be one of the best add-ons you could get for Kodi, but since then things have taken a turn for the worse, with dead stream and links becoming commonplace. That's where Exodus comes in. Created by the makers of Genesis, Exodus is already one of the most popular add-ons available for Kodi, and Kodi users are already saying it's one of the best. It's the starting point for a lot of new Kodi users, so it's worth downloading and installing to see the kind of content that you can expect.

5 Velocity

Source: http://fusion.tvaddons.ag
Zip: kodi-repos, english, repository. BlazeRepo.x.x.x.zip
Repository: Blazetamer's Repository, Video add-ons, Velocity

Velocity is one of the newest, best add-ons for Kodi, but it's already proving popular. Why? Because it's easy to use and brings with it a host of new content and increased stability. Better yet, it also comes in two flavours, so there's a Velocity Kids version for smaller Kodi users, too.

6 SALTS

Source: http://fusion.tvaddons.ag
Zip: kodi-repos, english, repository. tknorris.beta-x.x.x.zip
Repository: Tk Norris Release Repository, Video add-ons, SALTS

Developed by the same people that brought us 1channel.ch, SALTS stands for Stream All The Sources and that tells you pretty much all you need to know. Already tipped as a great alternative to the outgoing Genesis, SALTS is quick, easy to use and isn't hard to install. Once installed, you'll find it easy to find the content you want to watch.

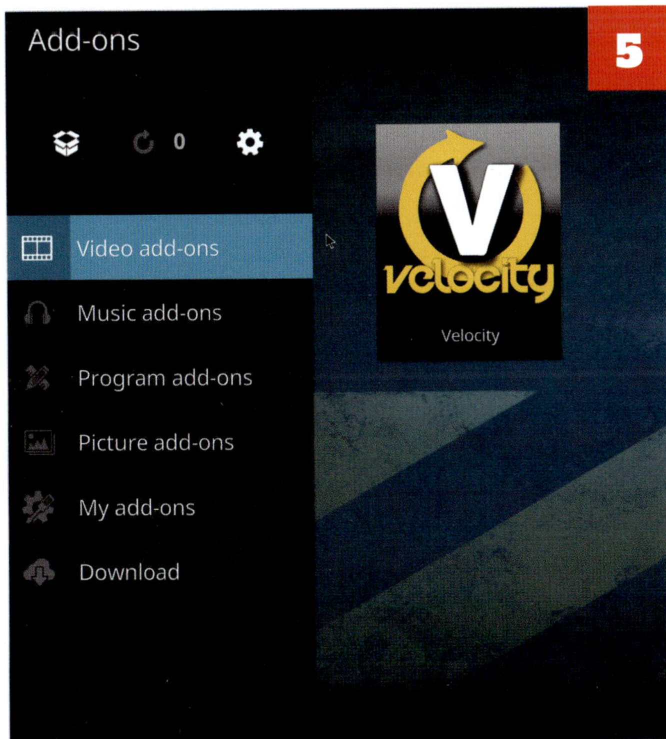

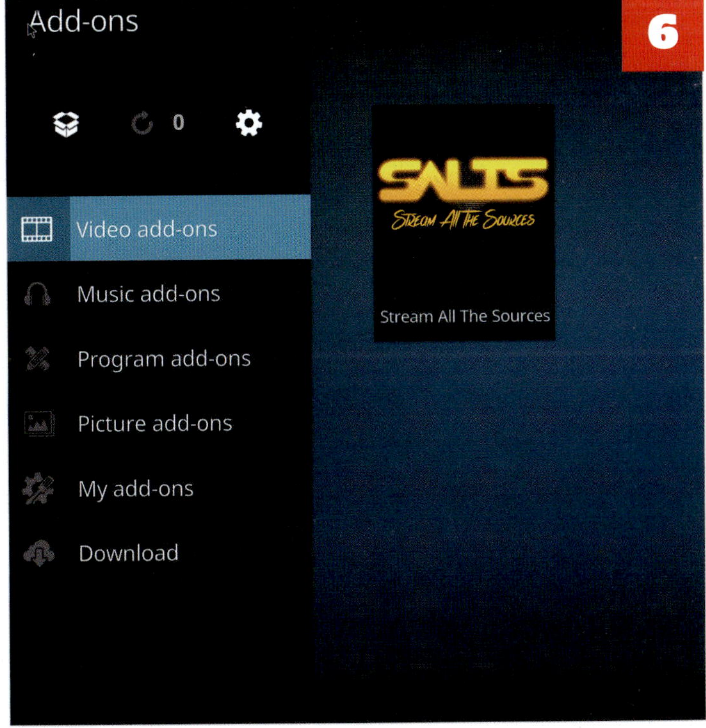

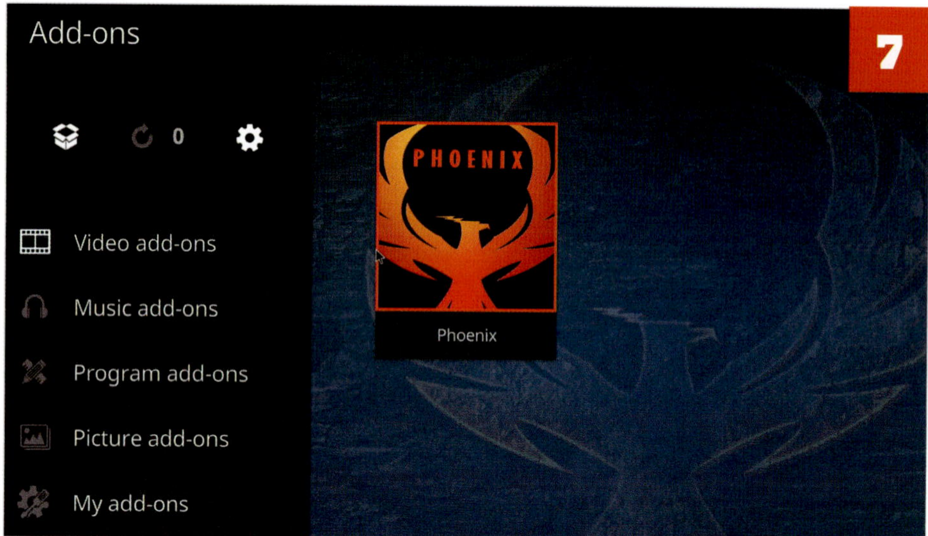

7 Phoenix

Source: http://fusion.tvaddons.ag
Zip: kodi-repos, english, repository. xbmchub-x.x.x.zip
Repository: TVADDONS.ag Addon Repository, Video add-ons, Phoenix

When it comes to the sheer quality and amount of content, Phoenix has to be at the very top of any list of addons. Made by the creators of Mashup – previously one of the best addons for Kodi – and supported by a dedicated team of developers, Phoenix lets users watch pretty much anything in pin-sharp quality. It takes seconds to download, and will even let you choose your streaming bitrate if you have a weak connection.

8 SpotiMC

Source: See below
Zip: repository.beta.emby.kodi-x.x.x.zip
Repository: Kodi Emby Beta Addons, Music add-ons, Spotify

Like it or not, Spotify has changed the way we think about music. For only £10 per month, it lets users enjoy a huge library of tracks, and even allows music fans to download content to listen to offline. Throw in a range of varied playlists to help you discover music and other neat features, and Spotify is one of the best streaming services you can get. SpotiMC brings all of the benefits of the streaming service to Kodi, and thanks to an easy-to understand UI, it's a must-have app for any Spotify user.

Installation is a bit of a pain, though. First, download the Zip file from bit.ly/SpotiMC (the download will start immediately). Now, select the Install from Zip file option and browse to the Zip file you downloaded, and select repository.beta.emby.kodi-x.x.x.zip. Then install as normal using the Repository information above. When you run the add-on for the first time, you'll be prompted to log in; you'll then need to confirm the action on the Spotify website using the browser window that pops up.

9 Bob Unrestricted

Source: http://noobsandnerds.com/portal
Zip: noobsandnerds_repo.zip
Repository: Noobs and nerds repository, Video add-ons, Bobr

Bob Unrestricted is a brand-new add-on, developed by part of the team that brought the Phoenix add-on. As with that plug-in, Bob brings you a ton of content, including TV shows, movies, music and sports. It works really well, with the content playing automatically and without any hassle.

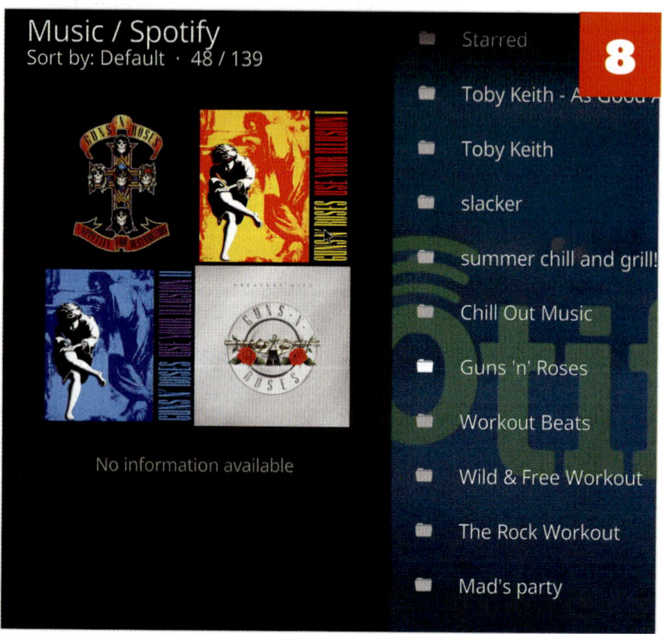

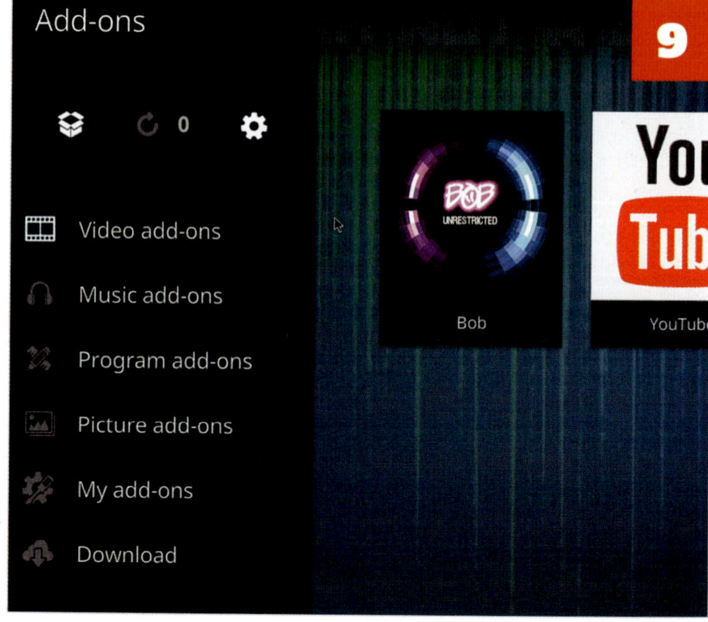

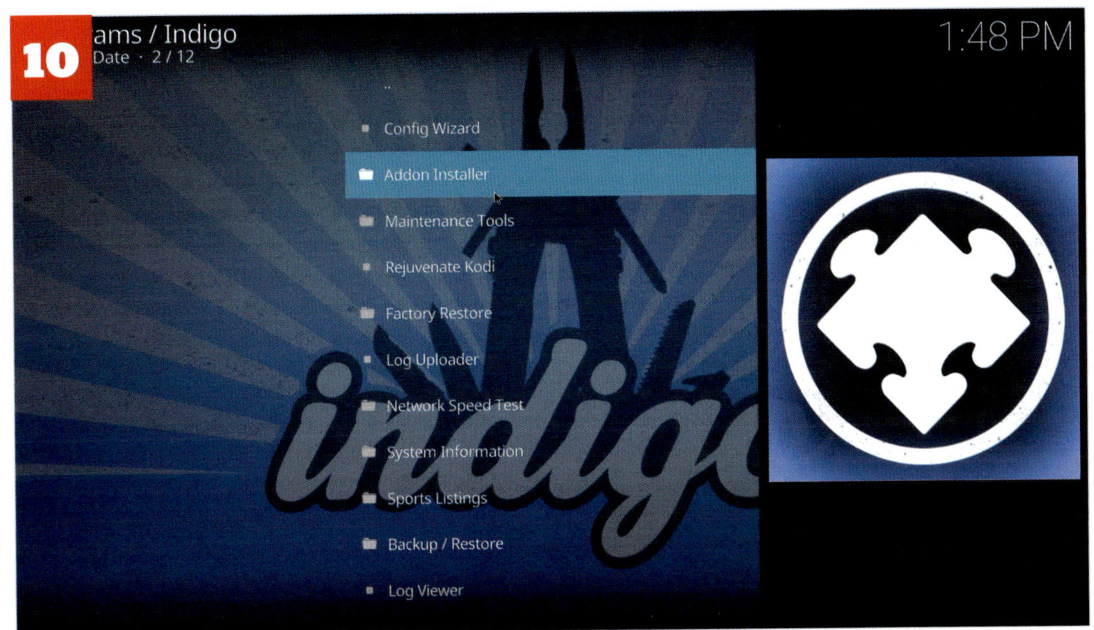

11 YouTube

As you'd expect, the largest video service in the world also has an addon for Kodi. Featuring more than a billion users – almost a third of the people on the internet – YouTube is still the number-one destination for mindless videos, insightful documentaries and everything in between. A must-have. YouTube is available through the official Kodi repository (see page 52).

12 Zem

Source: http://fusion.tvaddons.ag
Zip: kodi-repos, english, repository.shani-x.x.zip
Repository: Shanis Addon Repository, Video add-ons, Zem

Zem is a great addon for Pakistani and Indian news channel services, Bollywood films and has since expanded in becoming a great addon for sports channels – making it great for international users, too. For something different, give this add-on a go.

10 Addon Installer

Source: http://fusion.tvaddons.ag
Zip: begin-here, plugin.program.indigo-x.x.x.zip

Although Kodi supports extensions, they're not intuitive to set up – and that's where an installer comes in. Addon Installer is one of the best, and makes downloading extensions a slick experience. As well as providing a good selection of extensions, it keeps your new software in one place, making it simpler to update or delete them if needed. Once you've installed from the Zip file above, Addon Installer is available from My add-ons, Program add-ons.

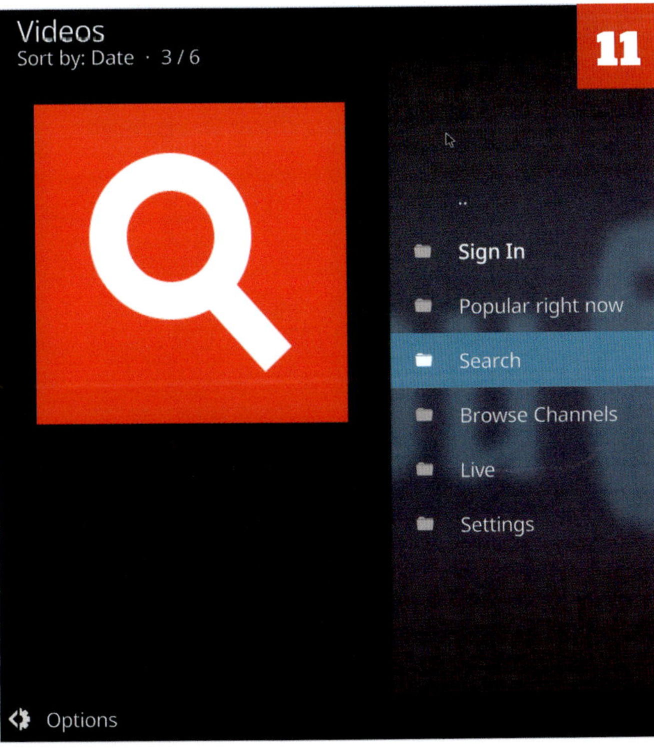

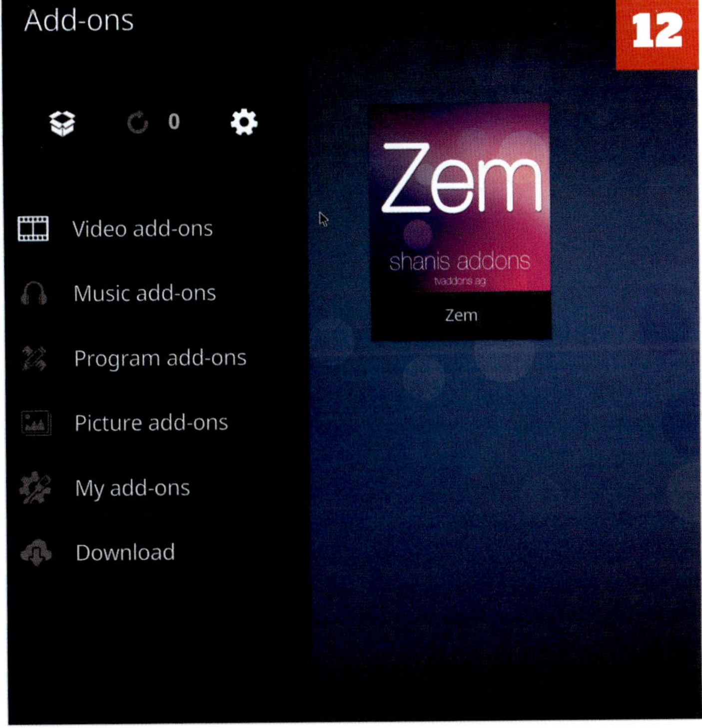

Chapter
5

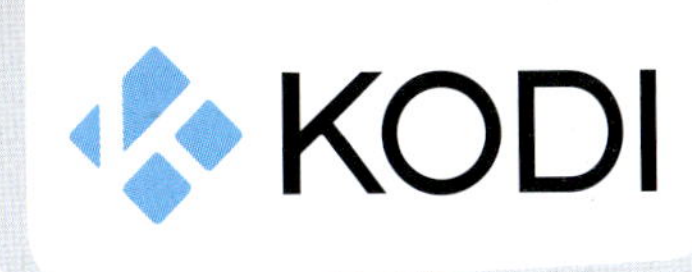

Media streamers

IN THIS SECTION

How to choose a media streamer

With more devices and a greater range of services than ever before, now's the time to invest in a media streamer and turn your unassuming living room television into a versatile smart TV

As good as Kodi is, it can be a pain to set up. There's an easier, cheaper method to watch TV and movies on your living room TV without being shackled to schedules: buy a dedicated media streamer.

Whether you just want to catch up on iPlayer or mainline Netflix for hours on end, there's almost certainly something to suit your needs, and often for less cash than you might think. Over the next pages we'll explain how to choose the media streamer that suits your needs, plus we've got round-ups of the current best models.

Form factor

You have two choices when it comes to form factor. The most common is the set-top box, but if this conjures images of bulky, blocky machines from the early 2000s, don't fret: the vast majority of these boxes are small enough to fit in the palm of your hand, let alone your lounge's AV cabinet.

This makes them, and the accompanying wires, easy to hide away. If you really don't have anywhere to put a set-top box, go for a stick, instead. These resemble slightly upsized USB sticks (except for the Google Chromecast, which looks more like a tiny hockey puck) and include an integrated HDMI connector so that they can plug directly into the back of your TV. They generally offer fewer external ports, so you won't find the USB sockets or microSD card slots that boxes have room for, but they're ideal for cable-cutting as they don't necessarily require a mains power source.

▲ A set top box (top) has more inputs and outputs, but a stick (left) may be more convenient.

Set top boxes are generally a little more powerful, but more expensive; sticks can be a little bit slower but are generally cheaper.

Services

It's important to note which streaming services a device can support; unfortunately, there still isn't a single media streamer that supports every single big-name service. UK terrestrial catch-up services are pretty well-covered, though, as is Netflix and YouTube. Amazon Instant Video is something of a wild card, as it's only really supported by Amazon's Fire TV products and the Roku products.

All that said, many of the streamers

▲ Make sure your media streamer has all of the services that you want.

have gained additional services since they initially launched, and it's certainly possible that we'll see greater proliferation in the future. It's in the manufacturers' interests, as well as consumers', that their media streamers can work with as many services as possible, so it's worth keeping an eye out for updates if you're not buying imminently.

Remote control

A media streamer isn't complete without some form of remote control. Other than the Chromecast, all the devices covered here include a dedicated remote in the box, and a few even support voice controls, so you can navigate through menus and search for shows, episodes and movies without needing to lift a finger. Many streamers have dedicated remote apps, which act as an alternative to the bundled remote.

As for the Chromecast, you control everything using the source app on your phone. For example, if you tap Pause on Netflix, the action will pause on your TV.

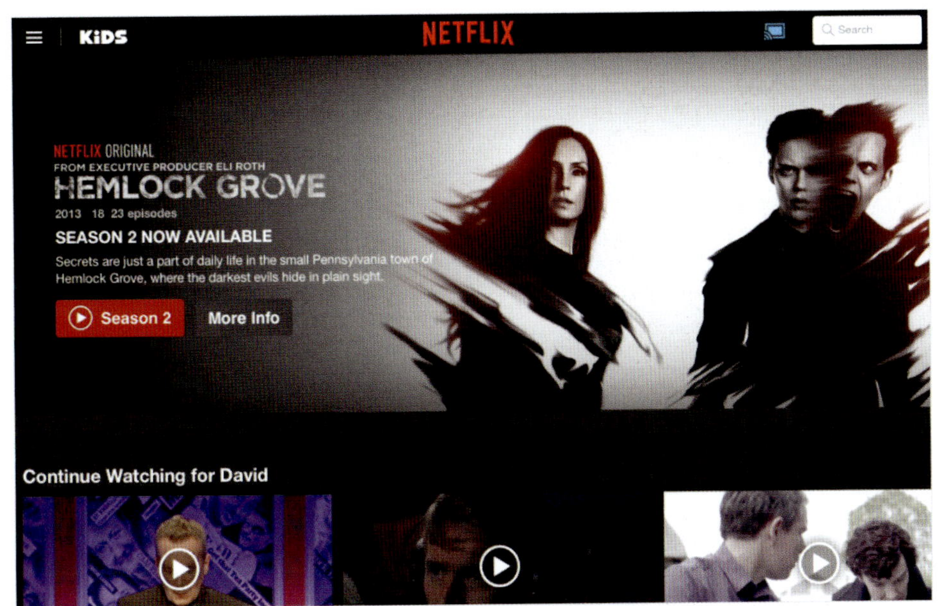

▲ The Chromecast is controlled via apps on your phone and has no physical remote.

Network support

Obviously, a media streamer will need to be connected to a network. Wi-Fi support is ideal, so that you don't need to connect any wires. However, you'll need a fairly strong Wi-Fi signal to get HD video.

Media streaming

As well as beaming in content from the internet at large, certain streamers allow you to view content saved on a DNLA (sometimes called UPnP) media server – provided it's on the same network, of course. Most NAS devices provide a compatible media server. Plex-compatible streamers work similarly; if you've got a PC or NAS elsewhere in the house, media saved on it can be accessed via the streamer.

Amazon Fire TV

With excellent app support and a choice of set-top box or TV stick, the Fire TV is hard to beat

Amazon Fire TV devices come as both a the cheap Fire Stick (Full HD) and the Fire TV set-top box, which supports 4K both in Amazon Instant Video and Netflix.

The square-shaped Fire TV is about the size of two decks of cards side-by-side, so it's easy to hide away in an AV cabinet. The Fire TV has built-in 802.11ac Wi-Fi and there's also a 10/100Mbit/s Ethernet port for wired connections should your router not be up to the task. There's also an optical S/PDIF connection.

The Fire TV Stick is the same size as a USB stick and plugs into your TV via its integrated HDMI port. It's powered by USB, and you'll need the supplied adaptor to provide enough power, as your TV's ports aren't good enough.

Both devices use the same type of remote. The Fire TV Stick has the option of a regular remote, or one with a microphone for voice control; the Fire TV just has the microphone option. This works well for hands-free searching though Amazon Prime Instant Video and Amazon's app store, but it won't work within apps.

The Fire TV's user interface is clean and well laid out, with distinct categories for Movies, TV, Games and Music. The 4K model's upgraded processor also makes navigating around the interface feel responsive and slick.

Naturally, there's a dedicated section for Prime Video. Its catalogue of movies and television shows is strong, although there are still films that you'll only find on rival services such as Netflix, and vice versa. The Amazon Fire TV has slick presentation and performance, and navigating its user interface was a pleasure.

You can also install apps from the Amazon App Store, including BBC News, Netflix, Vevo, Spotify and Dailymotion. With recent updates, the Fire TV now has all of the UK's terrestrial television catch-up services available as well.

While the Fire TV is extremely convenient for accessing your Amazon content, it's also possible to access your own content through DLNA media servers or AirPlay for watching on the big screen. Neither will work right out of the box, however, so you'll need to download and install separate Fire TV apps such as Plex or AirPlay/DLNA Receiver.

These will grant access to music, pictures or video on your other devices including tablets and desktops. The latter option is only a receiver so you'll still need to use a separate app or device to send the content to the Fire TV, but it can also be used to mirror your Apple device's display over AirPlay.

Some games are compatible with the included remote control, but the optional Fire TV Game Controller (£40) makes the Amazon Fire TV makes a much more viable gaming system.

If you have a 4K TV, the main Fire TV is the best media streamer to buy. For smaller TVs or where you want to save money, the excellent Fire TV Stick is a great choice with brilliant app support.

Apple TV 4th Gen

A high-quality media streamer with a big app store, this model is expensive but works with most services

There was always one thing missing from Apple TV: an App Store for downloading new services and customising the experience. That changed with the 4th generation model, released late last year.

It has the same 98mm square footprint, but new internal hardware means this latest model is 35mm tall, compared to 23mm on the old Apple TV. The A8 processor found in the iPhone 6 reappears here, providing more power for games and apps than the previous generation device, plus there's a choice of 32GB or 64GB of storage.

It's not so much bigger that you'll struggle to put it anywhere and it will sit neatly underneath a TV without getting in the way. It's brilliantly made, with a reassuringly heavy feel to it that gives the Apple TV a feeling of ruggedness.

Power, HDMI 1.4, 10/100Mbit/s Ethernet and a USB-C service port are found on the back, but the digital optical audio output is gone. The lack of Ultra HD support will be a real problem for some people, though 1080p is a decent compromise between quality and the internet bandwidth required to stream video. 802.11ac Wi-Fi is more than fast enough to stream Full HD content, particularly if you've got a matching 802.11ac Wi-Fi router running on the 5GHz band.

The interface will feel familiar to anyone that's used a previous generation Apple TV, despite running on the new tvOS operating system. Apps are still laid out in a grid, but the home screen looks a little bare. You get the basic range of Apple apps, but the rest is yours to fill from the App Store.

There are lots of apps, but some big names are missing. You've got Sky Now TV, but there's a serious lack of terrestrial catch-up services that have dedicated apps.

Where there aren't dedicated apps, you can use AirPlay in some situations. This lets you beam content from an iPhone to your Apple TV, controlling everything via the app. Amazon Instant Video is supported via this method, as is All4 and ITV Hub.

The Apple TV is particularly well-served for games, with popular iOS titles Lumino City, Crossy Road having made the jump to the big screen.

This is where the redesigned remote control really shines. With some games, the trackpad moves an on-screen cursor, while others – such as driving games and flight sims – use the built-in accelerometer.

The remote has an integrated battery, which is charged via the Lightning port and will last months at a time. The addition of a trackpad, extra buttons and Siri voice control improves the remote further. The trackpad makes zooming around the interface a lot easier, with velocity is taken into account; a quick swipe moves through lists faster than a slow one. It also fast-forwards or rewinds through content, but it's easy to brush against it when you pick up the remote, inadvertently skipping through your content.

Using the on-screen keyboard is a real chore, but the Siri microphone button lets you use your voice instead, searching for content using the universal search engine.

For some, the lack of Ultra HD might be a slight disappointment, given that the Amazon Fire TV box does support it; however, the Apple TV's fantastic design, voice controls and the potential for growth make it very appealing indeed.

Google Chromecast

Well-priced with excellent app support, this could be the media streamer for you if you don't mind controlling everything via apps

Google has two Chromecast options. The Ultra supports 4K video, but costs £90; the regular Chromecast supports Full HD video and costs just £30. Both work in the same way.

The Chromecast's tiny size and flexible HDMI cable means it's child's play to set up and keep out of sight. Power is still delivered through a microUSB port, ideally connected to a USB socket or nearby set top box or AV amp, though a power adaptor is included if these aren't available.

The Chromecast app has been improved as well. Where previously it was just used to connect the Chromecast to your wireless network and for screen mirroring, the new version is now more of a hub to find and access apps that support the Chromecast protocol for getting content to your big screen.

To use the Chromecast, you have to cast content from apps on our phone. From a supported app you simply tap the Chromecast button, select the Chromecast device you want to use and the content is sent from your smartphone or tablet to play on your TV. It doesn't actually stream from the control device to the Chromecast; as with AirPlay, the device talks to the Chromecast and tells it where it can access the stream from. The Chromecast then takes over playback duties, letting you use your PC, smartphone or tablet for any other job, unless you want to pause, rewind or fast-forward using the touchscreen controls.

The one downside of this method of control is that if your doorbell goes, you have to fiddle about with your phone to pause the action.

For movies, you're well-served by Netflix, Google Play Movies, Wuaki.tv and Blinkbox, and Android users (not iOS users, sadly) get access to Amazon Instant Video as well. Catch-up TV support has also improved since launch, with All 4 and ITV Hub joining iPlayer in offering Chromecast support. Demand 5, sadly, has not.

The best way to view your own video content via Chromecast is Plex, which you can run on either a network server or a computer. Its limited codec support, however, means you might need to transcode your videos into a format the Chromecast can support.

Chromecast isn't just about video, although that's clearly its primary purpose. In fact, any supported app can be cast to your TV, allowing you to send photos, audio and even the full onscreen app, interface and all. Games like The Big Web Quiz make excellent use of this; up to six players use the app on their phones to take part in an interactive quiz, with the results and questions appearing on the TV.

At its low price, the Google Chromecast is almost a no-brainer. Some may prefer to have a dedicated remote control and and on-screen interface, but for those who just want a cheap and convenient way of adding streaming services to your TV, the Chromecast is a solid choice.

Roku 3

Although a little old, the Roku 3 remains a powerful media streamer with lots of great apps available for it

he Roku 3 is an evolution of the Roku 2 XS, and shares its Fast Ethernet port, a Micro SD card slot and USB port, but loses its predecessor's A/V output. This means that you'll only be able to use the Roku 3 with HD TVs. Should you wish, you can use the USB port to play music, videos and photos from USB drives.

It's easy to set up – you'll need to create a Roku account on your PC or mobile device first, in order to link it to the device, but then you simply connect the box to your TV via HDMI cable and immediately start downloading channels. You only get a choice between 720p and 1080p, though.

Once set up, you can add more channels (read apps) to your Roku in the channel store. Many are free, but there are also a good few that require subscriptions (such as Netflix), or a one-off payment, like the Pac-Man and Galaga games.

The Roku 3 builds on the Roku 2 XS's great user interface design by having a scrollable menu on the left-hand side of the screen and a matrix of tiles that you can move through on the right-hand side of the screen. The left-hand list is used to move through categories and options such as Special Interest and Settings, while the tiles represent channels. The design certainly looks slick, with very high-quality graphics, and it's a breeze to navigate as well.

The Roku store also includes Plex, which makes accessing your own content from a local computer or NAS an easy process. The Plex channel on Roku right now isn't quite as nice to look at as on rival devices, but it is perfectly functional and constantly being improved.

Roku has also updated its boxes with universal search, so you can look for television shows, films, actors or directors across different Roku channels. This has made it significantly easier to find content to watch, and Roku says it will continue to add more services to its search. Roku Feed, where you can follow availability and pricing updates for specific movies, has also been added.

In terms of catch-up services, Roku boxes have all of the bases covered. There's BBC iPlayer, ITV Player, Demand 5 and All 4, so all of the terrestrial channels. You also have Netflix for subscription-based video-on-demand. Recently, Amazon Video was added, so you have access to Amazon Instant Video if you're an Amazon Prime subscriber – a rare feature outside of Amazon's own streamers.

Another neat feature of the Roku 3 is the headphone socket built into the remote control. Plugging in headphones mutes your TV, so you can listen without disturbing the rest of the house.

The remote control is a motion controller, just like the Roku 2 XS's (and Apple TV's) remote control, working just like a Wiimote. This makes it an ideal controller for games such as Angry Birds. You also have the option of using the Roku app on your smartphone or tablet to control your box.

Overall, the Roku 3 is not just an improvement on the Roku 2 XS, but is arguably the best media streamer around in terms of its range of content and ease of use.

Streaming sticks

Award	Recommended		
Manufacturer	Amazon	Google	Google
PRODUCT	FIRE TV STICK	CHROMECAST (2015)	CHROMECAST ULTRA (2015)
Hardware			
Form factor	Dongle	Dongle	Dongle
Audio inputs	None	None	None
Audio outputs	None	None	None
Video outputs	HDMI	HDMI	HDMI
USB port	microUSB (for power)	microUSB (for power)	microUSB (for power)
Internal storage	None	None	None
Expandable storage	None	None	None
Networking	802.11n	802.11ac	802.11ac
NFC	None	None	None
App support	Android, iOS	Android, iOS	Android, iOS
Dimensions	14x44x119mm	52x52x13.9mm	52x52x13.9mm
Weight	57g	34g	34g
Streaming			
Streaming formats	DLNA, Plex, UPnP	Chromecast, Via app: DLNA, Plex, UPnP	Chromecast, Via app: DLNA, Plex, UPnP
Streaming video	Amazon Instant Video, Netflix, Now TV	Amazon Instant Video, Google Play Movies 7 TV, Netflix, Now TV	Amazon Instant Video, Google Play Movies 7 TV, Netflix, Now TV
Catch-up TV	BBC iPlayer, All 4, ITV Hub	BBC iPlayer, ITV Hub, All 4	BBC iPlayer, ITV Hub, All 4
Buying information			
Price	£35	£30	£90

Set-top boxes

Award	Recommended	Recommended	Best Buy
Manufacturer	Amazon	Apple	Roku
Product	Fire TV with 4K Ultra HD	TV	3
Hardware			
Form factor	Box	Box	Box
Audio inputs	None	None	None
Audio outputs	S/PDIF	None	Headphone out
Video outputs	HMDI	HDMI	HDMI
USB port	1x USB2	USB Type-C (for service)	1x USB3
Internal storage	8GB	32/64GB	512MB
Expandable storage	microSD	None	microSD
Networking	802.11n	802.11ac, Ethernet, Bluetooth 4.0	802.11n, Ethernet
App support	Android, iOS	iOS	Android, iOS, Windows Phone
Dimensions	115x115x17mm	98x98x35mm	89x89x25mm
Weight	281g	425g	142g
Streaming			
Streaming formats	AirPlay, DLNA, Plex	AirPlay, Via app: DLNA, Plex, UPnP	DLNA, Plex, UPnP
Streaming video	Amazon Instant Video, Netflix, Now TV	Amazon Instant Video (via app), Netflix, Now TV	Amazon Instant Video, Google Play Movies, Netflix, Now TV
Catch-up TV	BBC iPlayer, All 4, ITV Hub	BBC iPlayer, All 4 (via app)	BBC iPlayer, ITV Player, Demand 5, All 4
Buying information			
Price	£80	£139/£179	£70

Stream to any device with VLC Media Player

We show you how to use VLC Media Player to stream music and video across all your entertainment devices.

VLC (www.videolan.org) is a free, open source media player that can play most audio and video files, as well as DVDs and audio CDs. But it can also do lots more than that. You can use the software as a hub to get media from your hard drive (or anywhere else for that matter), on to any other device, including Google Chromecast, Apple TV, iPhones, iPads, Android devices, and more. For this project we'll look at what you can stream to using VLC, and explain how to do it.

Stream videos over your network

If you want to remotely watch videos stored on your PC, VLC Media Player is perfect for the task. The setup process is easy enough, once you know how. Install the software on both the host (the computer where your videos are stored) and the remote PC you want to watch on. On the host PC, find your IP address by clicking Start, typing CMD and pressing the Enter key. Type ipconfig into the command prompt and press Enter. Make a note of the address next to IPv4 Address. With that done, return to VLC and go to Media, Stream. Select a video to play, and click the Stream button. A wizard will open. Click Next, choose HTTP in the New destination drop-down box, and click Add. Click Next, then Next again, and finally click Stream. On the remote PC (the one you plan to watch on) go to Media, Open Network Stream and enter http://ipaddress:8080 (using the other computer's actual IP address). If the video doesn't play, you'll need to make sure that the Windows firewall on either computer isn't blocking the stream.

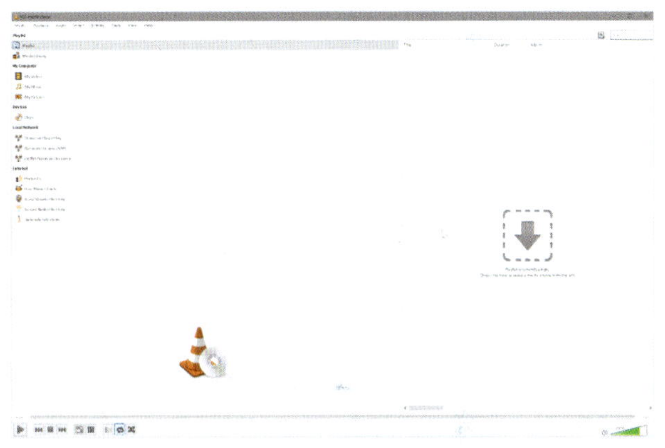

▲ The nightly build of VLC for Windows has a more polished look and introduces several new features, including Chromecast support

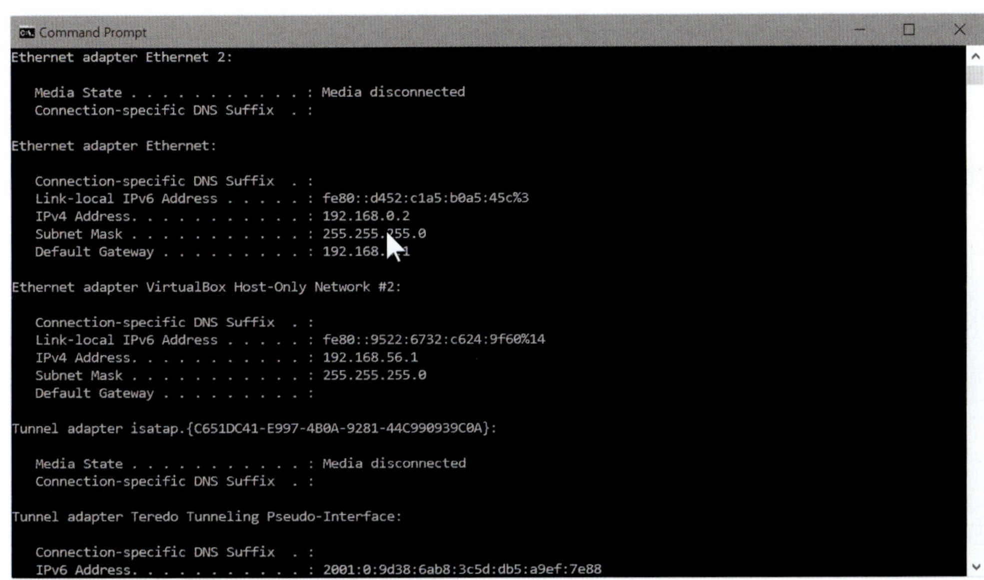

▲ To stream video over your network you'll need to find the host system's IP address using the IP Config command

Stream to Chromecast from Android

Like the PC version of VLC, the Android app doesn't come with native Chromecast support. You can still stream movies from your Android phone or tablet to the Chromecast,

▲ The Google Home app lets you connect to your Chromecast and find things to watch

however.

First, install the Chromecast app, now called Google Home (bit.ly/ghome411) on your phone or tablet, and pair it to your Chromecast. Once you've done that, install and run VLC for Android (bit.ly/vlca411), and start playing the video file you want to watch. Open the Chromecast app, tap the menu button and select Cast screen/audio. Follow the instructions to cast your Android device's screen to your Chromecast, then go back to VLC and switch the video to fullscreen. You can now start enjoying it on your TV.

Watch videos on iOS

VLC Streamer (bit.ly/vlcs411) is an independently-developed program that lets you stream movies stored on your computer to any Apple mobile device. You need to run the Streamer Helper on your computer (Windows, Linux and MacOS are supported) and then install the relevant app on your iPhone or iPad (bit.ly/stream411). The free version is ad-supported but should be your first port of call to make sure it does everything you need it to. If you want to go ad-free, you can upgrade to the full version for £2.29. This version also includes an app for Apple Watch.

Stream videos to Apple TV

Apple TV offers a decent selection of its own streaming media apps, but doesn't let you easily watch your own movies and TV shows. As you might expect, VLC can solve that problem for you.

All you need to do is open the app store on your Apple TV and download and install VLC for Mobile. This runs on the fourth-generation Apple TV – previous devices are not supported. Launch the app and open the Local Network tab. Use the Apple TV remote to browse through any media files stored on other devices and computers on your network (you may need to log in to them). You can then select and play any video files. They should run full screen.

Swipe down on the Apple Remote's touchpad to display the menu. From here you'll be able to make changes to the audio settings, manage any subtitles and change the playback speed.

If you don't have any PCs or NAS drives with media on them, you can use VLC for Mobile's remote playback functionality instead. Run the app on Apple TV and select the Remote Playback tab. Select Enable Remote Playback. Make a note of the IP address that appears on screen, and then open a web browser on a PC on your local network, and enter the IP address. Drag and drop a video you want to watch on Apple TV onto the remote playback window, or click the plus button and browse for your file that way. You can also enter a URL if you want to stream a web video. Tap the play button and the video should start playing on your Apple TV.

Finally, if you select the Network Stream option on your Apple TV you can enter a web video URL to play. VLC requires the hidden URL of the actual video itself, rather than a link to video page, so you may need to do some digging around to find it.

To do this, right-click a video and see if there's any way to get the link, or right-click the web page and select 'View page source'. You may find the video link there – but you will probably have to do some serious hunting. For that reason, you'd be better off sticking with the other two streaming methods we've recommended instead.

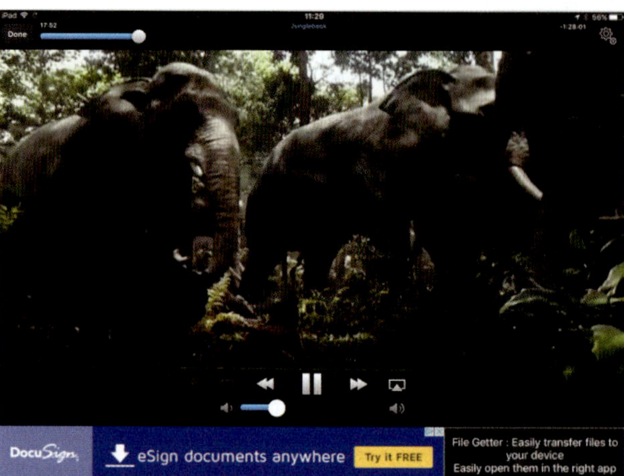

▲ The free version of VLC Streamer has adverts at the bottom, which you might find distracting

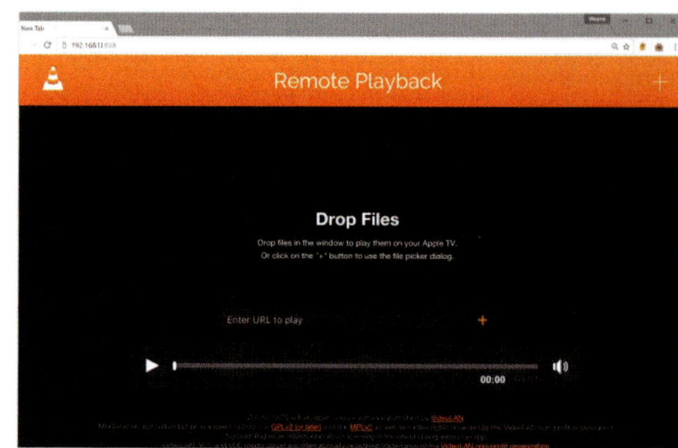

▲ The easiest way to stream video to an Apple TV using VLC is through the Remote Playback feature

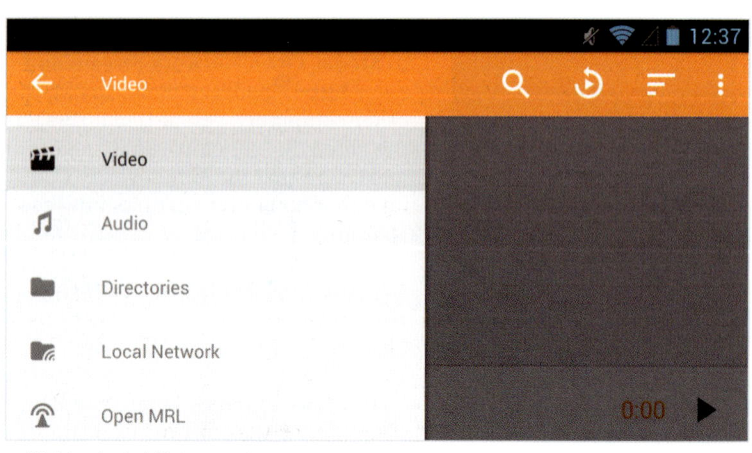

▲ VLC for Android lets you play video on your phone and cast it to the big screen

Chapter
6

Unlock internet content

IN THIS SECTION

How to watch US Netflix

You can tune into US Netflix with your UK account details, unlocking loads of extra content for free

One of the best things about Netflix is that the US version had a much bigger catalogue of shows than the UK, due to the way that international licensing works. Brilliantly, Netflix serves the catalogue based on the country you're in: so, a UK user in the US gets the full American inventory. It used to be fairly trivial to trick Netflix into thinking that you were in the US, rather than the UK, using a Virtual Private Network (VPN) or proxy server. However, Netflix has recently started to block people using VPNS and proxies, giving the error message, "You seem to be using an unblocker or proxy. Please turn off any of these services and try again."

This error message has been seen more and more, and while the unblocke services all said at the start that they would find a way around the issue, precious few have done so, and more are getting shut down all of the time. Fortunately, we have a solution.

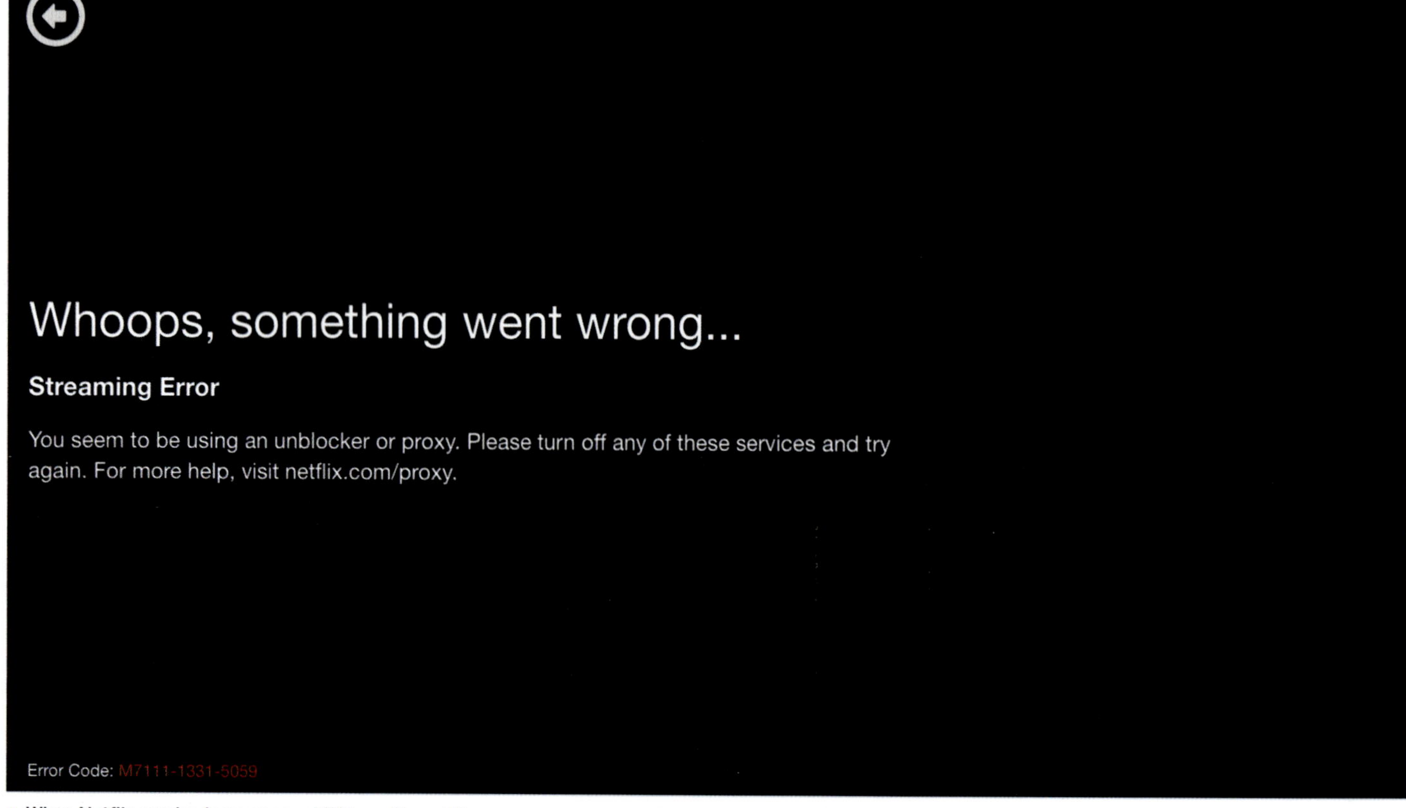

▲ When Netflix cracks down on your VPN, you'll see this message.

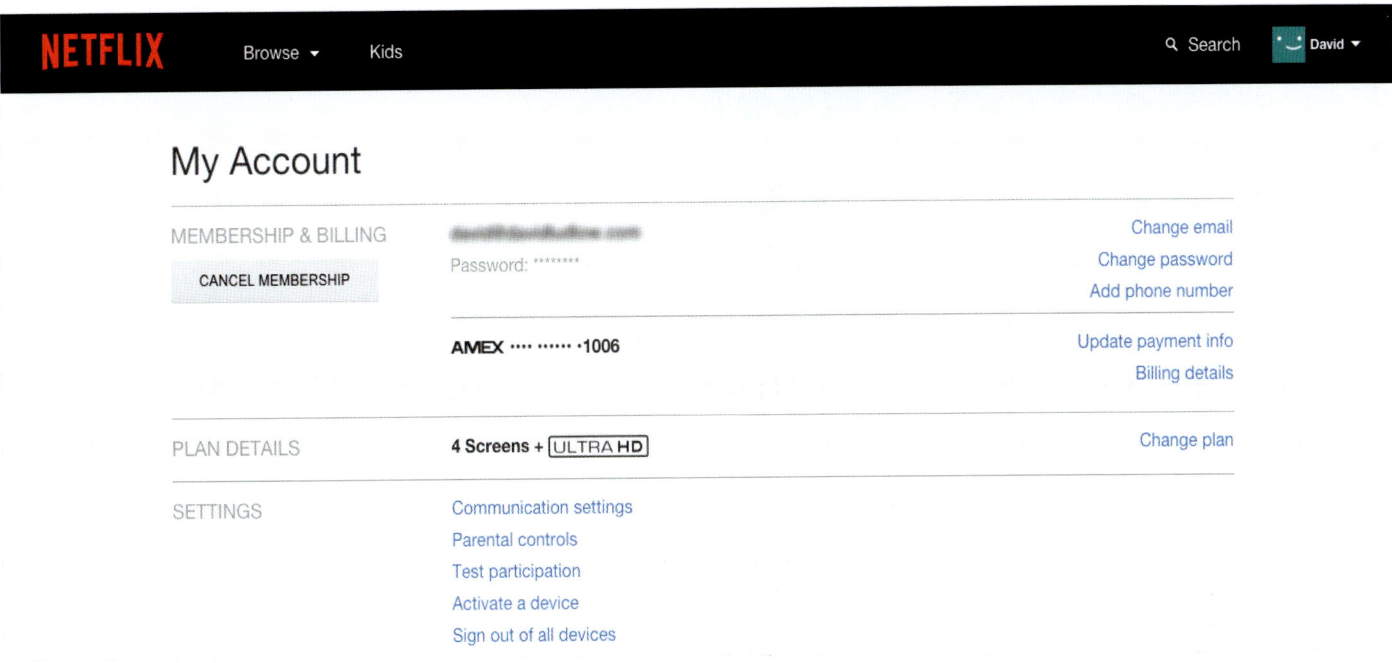

▲ You may need to sign out of Netflix on all devices, before you can watch US content

Why you might need a full VPN

The problem with most unblocker services is that they're smart VPNs, which you use by changing a device's Domain Name Service (DNS) server settings. DNS is the part of the internet that turns human-readable addresses, such as www.google.co.uk, into machine-readable IP addresses (the unique location of a computer on the internet). Using a smart VPN, when your computer tries to connect to Netflix, the new DNS server hands out the IP address of a tunnel, which your computer then uses to send its data to the US.

It's a clever system, as only traffic to do with hiding your location is sent via the US, while actual streaming and other websites are delivered as normal. The downside is that Netflix has become smarter with its detection, making it easier to block you from accessing its servers.

With a full VPN, it's different because all of your traffic is sent through the tunnel, so everything pops out in the US. This makes it harder for Netflix to detect, as your computer appears as though it actually is in a different country. However, Netflix can and will block IP addresses it suspects as being used in a VPN from joining its service, so this is not a guaranteed fix.

Another downside is that a VPN blocks you from running UK-specific services, such as BBC iPlayer. Finally, you can only run a VPN directly on devices that can run software, such as a PC or phone; Smart TVs and games consoles can't install the software, so you'll need to have a router that supports the VPN and tunnel all of your traffic. The good news about the latter option is that you can then use any device, including the Apple TV, a smart TV or Chromecast. We'll show you how to set up a router later in this guide.

Both Buffered (www.buffered.com) and ExpressVPN (www.expressvpn.com) both have proved reliable in the past, able to beat the Netflix ban. ExpressVPN is our preferred choice, as it's a little easier to use.

IMPORTANT: AirPlay and Chromecast

If you want to use AirPlay to send video from your iPhone, iPad or Mac to your Apple TV, or use an iPhone or Android device to beam content to a Chromecast, then all of your devices need to be connected to a VPN. If only your iPhone was, for example, then the Apple TV would be unable to connect to the video stream that you send it. For this reason, you'll need to have a router configured with VPN access (see page 78).

Sign out of Netflix

First, sign out of Netflix on all devices. The easiest way to do this is to go to www.netflix.com and sign in. At the top-right of the screen hover over your Profile image and click Your Account. Under Settings click Sign out of all devices and click the Sign Out button to continue.

How to use a VPN with Windows, Mac, iPhone or Android

If you just want to use one device to access American Netflix, then the easiest solution is just to install the client on your device. This differs depending on whether you have a PC or Mac, or a smartphone. I'll take each one in turn, so you can see how to configure them.

Windows or OS X (macOS) - Buffered

If you've got a desktop computer or laptop, you need to download the Buffered VPN client and install it on your computer. In both cases, you'll be prompted to install a driver after the main software has been installed, so allow this. Once done and you've launched the client, log in with your Buffered account details and then choose the country you want your computer to appear in: there are East Coast and West Coast servers. Once your computer is connected, fire up Netflix, log

▲ Buffered VPN lets you choose which server to connect to: try a few if you're having problems.

▲ Express VPN has loads of servers, so change to a different one if you can't connect.

in and you'll have access to the different catalogue. If you get an error, sign out of Netflix, disconnect the VPN, then reconnect and log back into Netflix. You can also try switching servers, but we've had no problems with either US servers.

Windows or OS X (macOS) - ExpressVPN

If you've got a desktop computer or laptop, you need to get an ExpressVPN account and download and install the software on your computer. When you run the software for the first time, you have to enter your Activation Code, which is listed under My Subscriptions on the ExpressVPN page. This will then activate the service, so you can click Start using the app to continue. You can click the big power button to turn the VPN on, but this will pick a smart location, based on speed (for us, it was Berkshire in the UK). This is useful if you want to browse the internet privately, but if you want to watch US Netflix, you need to use the Location Picker and button and choose a US destination. This gives you a list of servers to choose from, with the default list filtered by Recommend servers; you can click All if you want to see the massive range of servers. The latter option is useful if you can't get American Netflix with a Recommended server. Double-click your selection to connect. Once you see that the VPN is connected, you can fire up Netflix in your browser and watch US content: if you've got problems, log out of Netflix, restart your browser and try again; if this doesn't work, try switching location in ExpressVPN. To disconnect just click the big power button.

Android and iOS - Buffered

Using Android or iOS is a little fiddlier, as Buffered doesn't have its own client, but instead uses the OpenVPN client instead. You can get OpenVPN Connect in the Apple App Store for iPhones and iPads, and OpenVPN in the Google Play Store. You then need to download the right configuration script from Buffered (there's one for each country and two for the US, with East and West Coast options) and install this on your phone. Buffered's

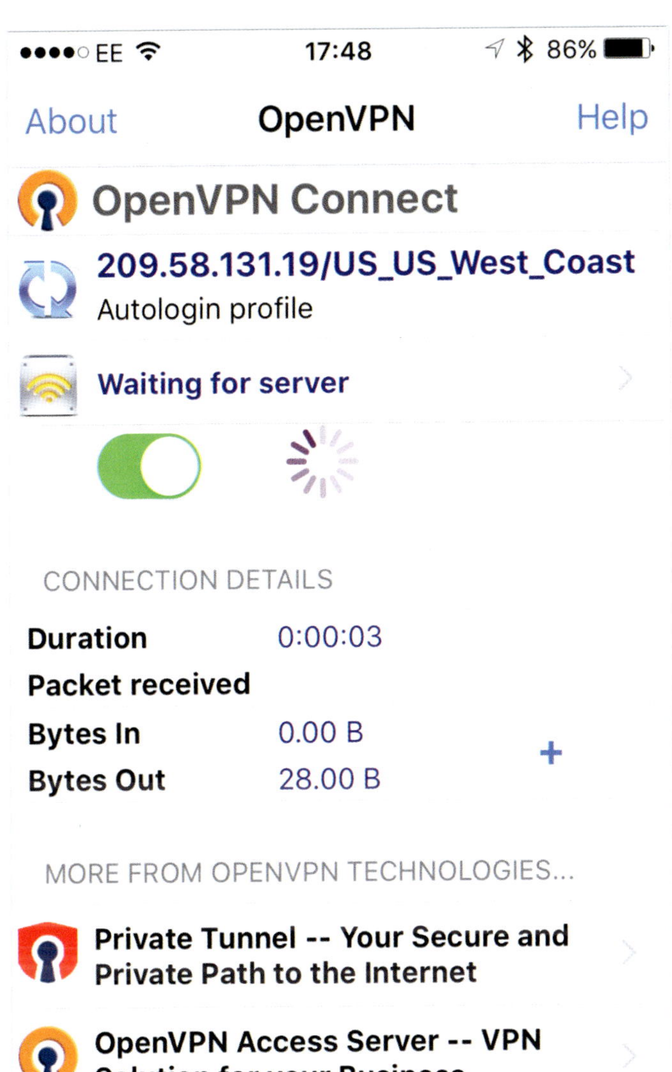

▲ Buffered uses the OpenVPN client, which makes mobile configuration a little tricky.

▲ ExpressVPN's smartphone client is excellent and really easy to use.

tutorials (available on www.buffered.com) are very good, so follow them for the exact instructions. Switching region in the future is time-consuming, though.

Android and iOS - Express VPN

You can get ExpressVPN for iOS on the app store and ExpressVPN for Android on the Google Play store. Once downloaded, open the app, sign in with your ExpressVPN details and follow the on-screen instructions to get the app working. Once signed in, tap Location and then choose where in the US you want to be located. There are Recommended servers as default, but you can click All if you're having problems and want to pick a more obscure server.

Running a VPN on a router for all devices

If you've got a device that doesn't let you install a VPN, then you need to run a VPN on a router instead, using ExpressVPN. The only problem is that most routers don't have the required support. Instead, you have two options. First, you can use a router that supports the open-source DD-WRT firmware. This doesn't have to be expensive, as you can pick up routers quite cheaply that support this (the Linksys E1200 N300 Wireless-N Router costs £25 from Amazon). See the DD-WRT website for full instructions on install the new firmware (www.dd-wrt.com). Secondly, you can buy router that runs ExpressVPN's custom software. The Linksys WRT1200AC costs $250 (around £210) from www.flashrouters.com.

Whichever your choice, you should run your VPN as a second router. This means that your normal devices connect to the internet properly, but you can choose to connect to your Netflix Wi-Fi for when you want to watch US shows. You'll need a router with an Ethernet WAN port to do this.

Configure DD-WRT router

Don't plug your router into your home network yet. Instead, power your router on and plug a computer into it via Ethernet.

Now, you need to configure your new router, and connect to the web-

Setup | Wireless | Services | Security | Access Restrictions | NAT / QoS | Administration | Status

Basic Setup | DDNS | MAC Address Clone | Advanced Routing | VLANs | Networking | EoIP Tunnel

WAN Setup

WAN Connection Type

Connection Type	Automatic Configuration - DHCP

Optional Settings

Router Name	DD-WRT
Hostname	
Domain Name	
MTU	Manual 1492
STP	Enable Disable

Network Setup

Router IP

Local IP Address	192 . 168 . 1 . 1
Subnet Mask	255 . 255 . 255 . 0
Gateway	0 . 0 . 0 . 0
Local DNS	0 . 0 . 0 . 0

Network Address Server Settings (DHCP)

DHCP Type	DHCP Server
DHCP Server	Enable Disable
Start IP Address	192.168.1. 2
Maximum DHCP Users	98
Client Lease Time	1440 min

Help more...

Automatic Configuration - DHCP:
This setting is most commonly used by cable operators.

Hostname:
Enter the hostname provided by your ISP.

Domain Name:
Enter the domain name provided by your ISP.

Local IP Address:
This is the LAN-side IP address of the router.

Subnet Mask:
This is the subnet mask of the router.

DHCP Server:
Allows the router to manage your IP addresses.

Start IP Address:
The address you would like to start with.

Maximum DHCP Users:
You may limit the number of addresses your router hands out. 0 means only predefined static leases will be handed out.

Time Settings:

▲ You need to give your DD-WRT router a new IP address.

based management page, which should be http://192.168.1.1. Click on Setup and scroll down to IP address under Network Setup. Look at the IP address, which should be 192.168.1.1. If this is the same IP address as your main router, you'll run into problems, so you need to change this: we recommend changing it to 192.168.2.1. Click Save and then Apply. Disconnect from your router and then reconnect. Now go to the web-based management page, remembering to connect to http://192.168.2.1 if you changed its IP address. Under Setup, change the Connection Type to Automatic Configuration - DHCP, then click Save, and then click Apply.

Next, click Wireless and configure the wireless networks, so that they make sense: we used the same name as our regular Wi-Fi network, but appended '-Netflix' to the end. Click Save and Apply. Now, you can connect your Netflix router to your existing router. To do this, use an Ethernet cable to connect your DD-WRT router's WAN port into a spare Ethernet LAN port on your main router. When you connect to your Netflix network, you'll be able to get internet access, so it's time to set up your VPN.

You now need to configure the OpenVPN client on your router, so that you can connect to US Netflix. We recommend following ExpressVPN's DD-WRT tutorial (bit.ly/expressvpnrouter), as it shows you exactly what to do. You'll need to download the matching configuration files for the server you want your router VPN to connect to. We recommend using the VPN app (see above) to find a server that works, and then download matching profiles on the ExpressVPN website, under the Linux/Routers Manual Configuration for OpenVPN section. If you skip this step, be warned, as changing regions on your router is a painful and time-consuming process.

And, read the instructions carefully, being aware that your DD-WRT interface may have options in a slightly

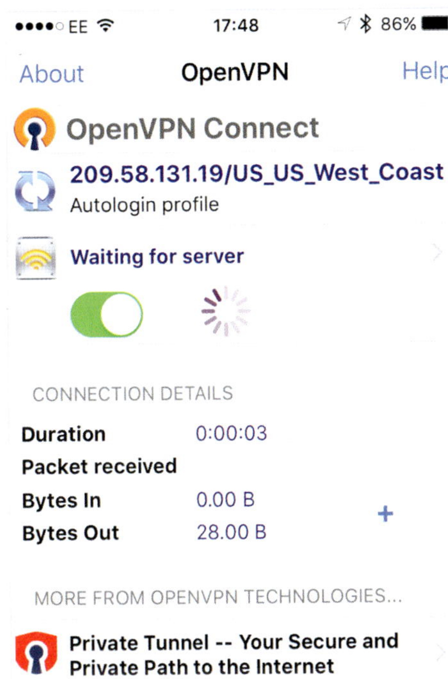

different order. You must do everything EXACTLY as it appears in the tutorial or you will get errors and won't be able to connect. Once you've made the changes click Save and Apply, then click Status, OpenVPN. When it says 'SUCCESS' and you see a 'Remote Address', the VPN is connected. It can take up to a minute to connect, so give it time and refresh the page to make sure. If you can't connect, then check the tutorial and your settings carefully.

Now, from any device at all, connect to your Netflix Wi-Fi router and fire up Netflix. You should get US Netflix, although if you don't, don't panic, just log out of Netflix and log back in to try it again. If you want to switch regions back to the UK, just switch back to your regular Wi-Fi network; if you set up DD-WRT as your only router, you'll have to go to Services, VPN and disable the OpenVPN client (you can just re-enable it next time you want US Netflix).

Use an ExpressVPN router

If you splash out on an ExpresVPN router, things are much easier. Plug the router's WAN port into on of your main router's LAN ports using an Ethernet cable. Now, connect a computer to the new router and follow the provided instructions to connect to the router's main interface (you can use the web address, http://expressvpnrouter.com). Log in and click VPN, ExpressVPN Account. Enter your activation code into the box. Now click on VPN connection and select your location: we recommend using the app on a PC to find a location that works for US Netflix first. However, changing region is easy so you can skip this step.

To change the Wi-Fi network name and password, click on Network and then Wi-Fi. Click the Edit button next to the network you want to change (there will most likely be one 2.4GHz network and one 5GHz). Edit the network name and password and then click Save & Apply.

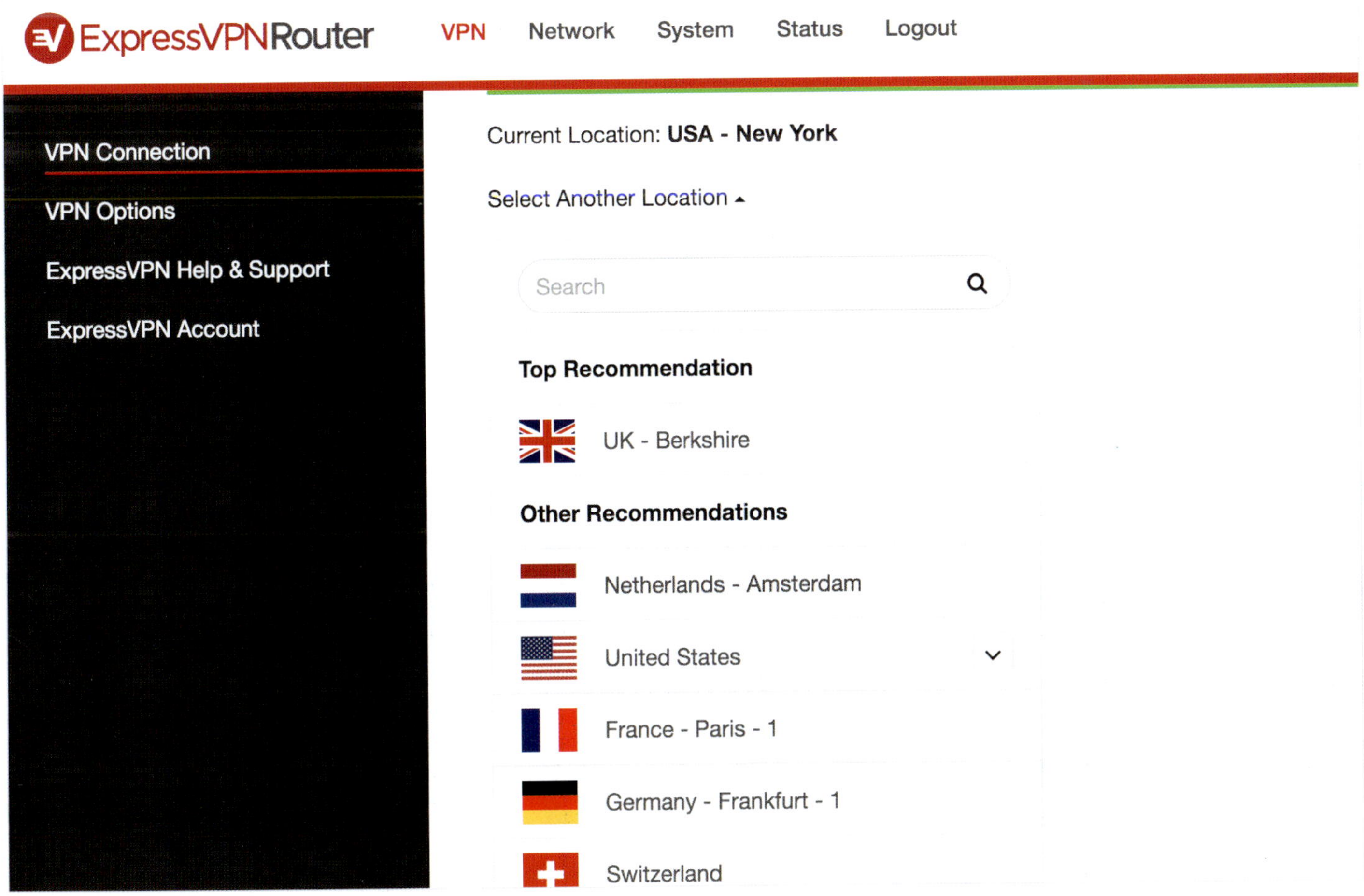

▲ The ExpressVPN router might be comparatively expensive, but it makes it really easy to connect any device to US Netflix.

How to watch UK TV abroad

When you go on holiday, you can lose access to all of your favourite content, unless you follow our top guide

In the UK, we're spoilt for great TV. Between the BBC, ITV, Channel 4, Channel 5, Freeview and Sky, there are literally hundreds of hours of content to keep you entertained. Thanks to web-based catch-up TV services like iPlayer there's no reason to miss out on your favourite shows if you aren't able to watch them live. It's not quite so simple if you find yourself out of the country, however; almost every service blocks access to foreigners based on their IP address.

Thankfully, there are plenty of quick, easy, and most importantly free ways to make sure you don't miss that crucial

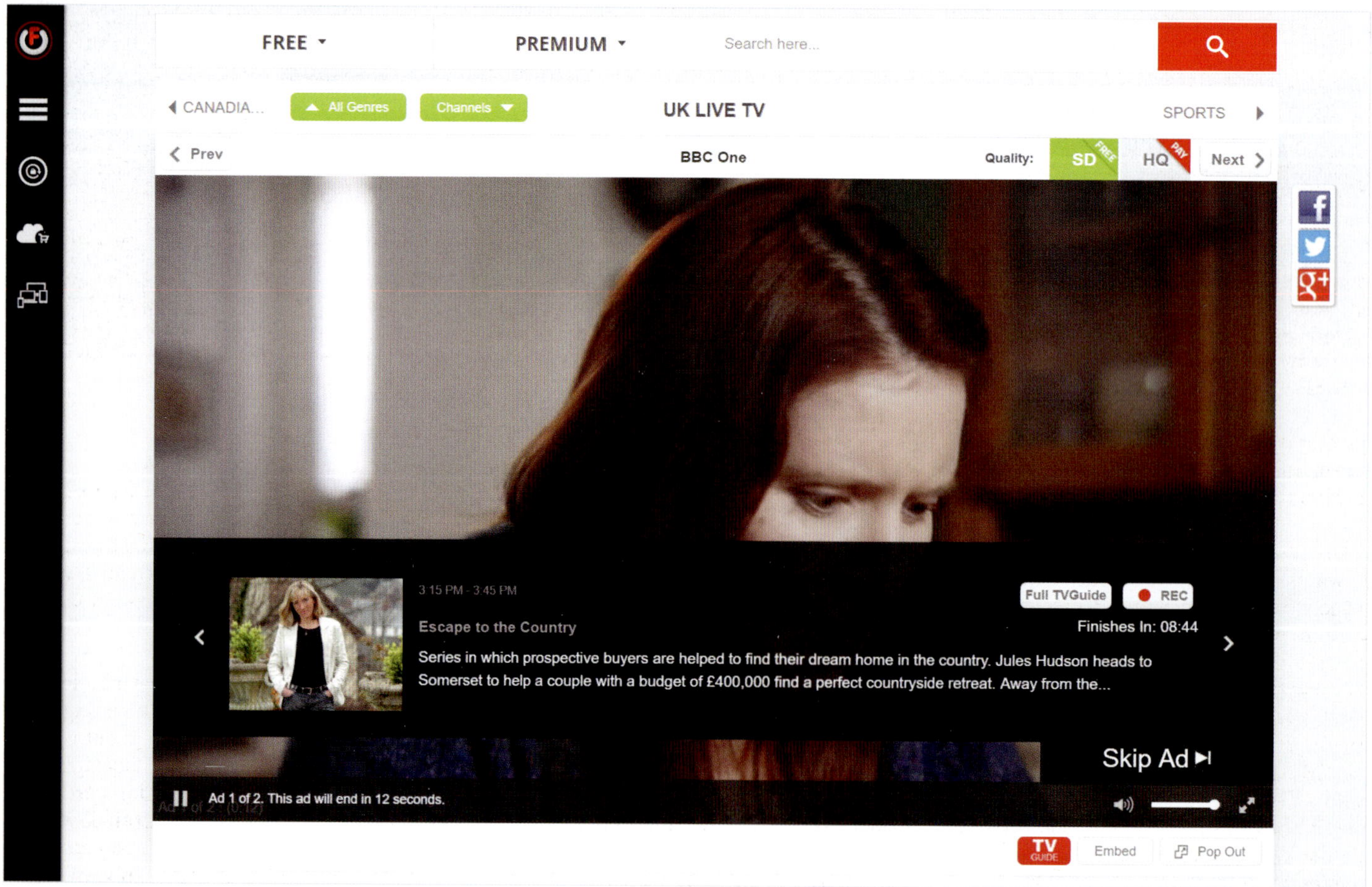

▲ FilmOn TV gives you access to UK live TV streams.

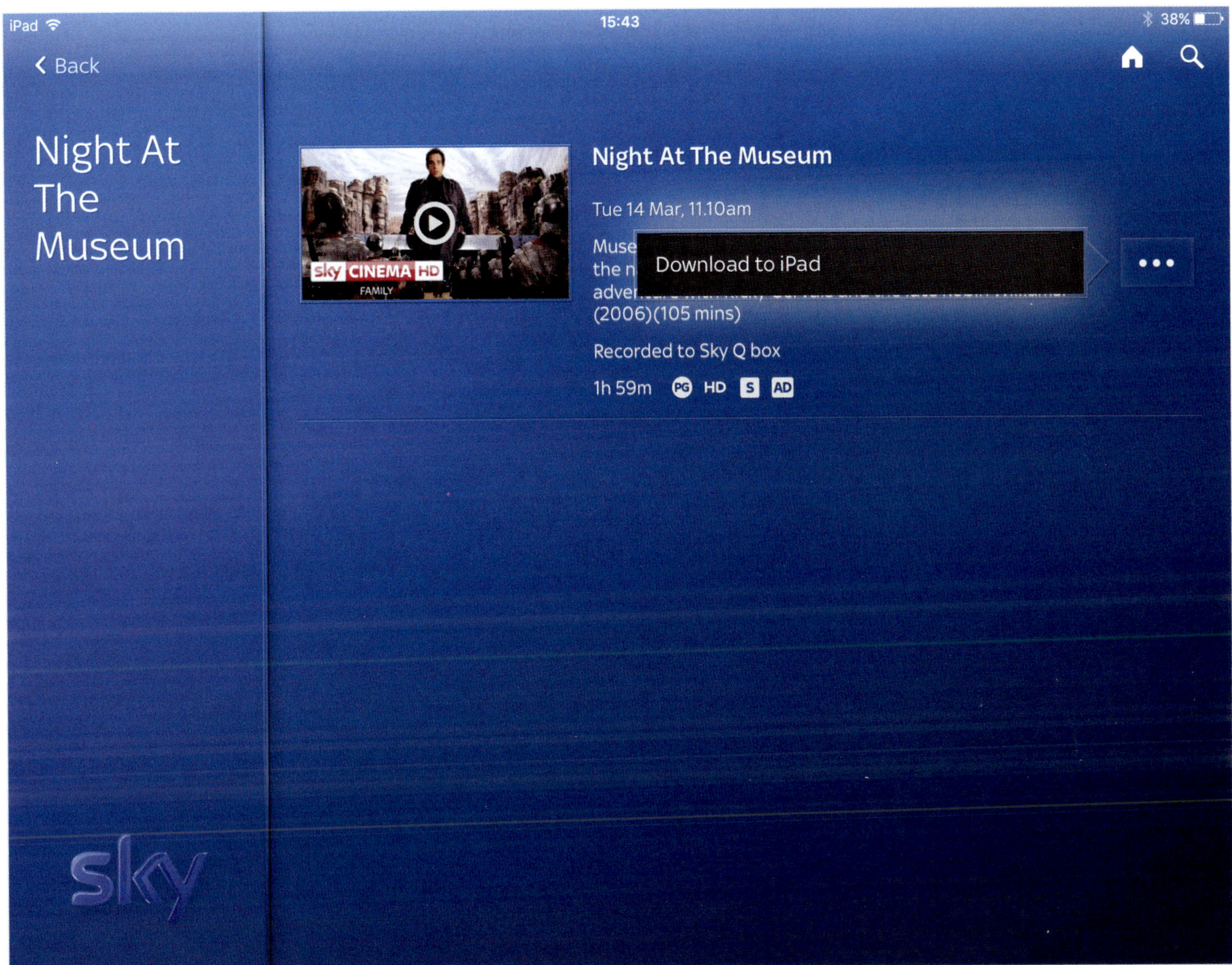

▲ You can download shows to your tablet before you go away.

episode when you're away on business or out on holiday. We've listed a few of the best below.

Live TV

To watch live UK TV from anywhere in the world using your web browser, without any need to install software or browser plugins, you can head to FilmOn TV (www.filmon.com). It will let you watch 26 different free-to-air channels, including BBC One, BBC Two, BBC News and CBBC, ITV1, Channel 4, E4, Channel 5 and a few other Freeview channels for free. It works using flash video embedding but also has a mobile site for tuning in on a tablet or smartphone. Unfortunately, broadcasts are only available for free in standard definition, and you have to pay if you want HD. Picture and sound quality isn't fantastic either, but it certainly beats missing an important football match or news bulletin.

Alternatively, WatchBritishTV (watchbritishtv.com/live-tv) includes live streams of the main channels, including Film4 and Dave, which FilmOnTV lacks. If also has on-demand streams of recent shows around six hours after broadcast. While these are not officially provided by the boradcasters and aren't properly categorised by channel or genre, they're easy to search for by name. This provides a somewhat effective alternative for 4OD, which has recently been particularly good at detecting overseas connection attempts, even from behind VPNs.

You'll need to subscribe to use WatchBritishTV's service, but its basic subscription service is free. We were particularly please to find that, although it shows its own logo on its streams, it doesn't superimpose advert banners.

Catch-up TV

The BBC only makes iPlayer available to UK-based license fee payers, meaning if you're out of the country you're out of luck. The same applies to the Sky Go and Sky Q services, which is a serious problem if you're missing out on the football while on holiday. If you're prepared, you can download BBC iPlayer shows to your phone or tablet before you go and you can

do the same for Sky if you've got a Sky Go Extra account or have Sky Q. If you're not that prepared, you can get around the issue with a VPN, although, for Sky Go or Sky Q you need a registered device with you.

Use a VPN

A Virtual Private Network (VPN) tunnels your network traffic, so that it appears to be coming from a different country. If you wanted to watch US Netflix in the UK, for example, you would use a VPN to tunnel your traffic to the US. The same kind of technique works in reverse, too, letting you tunnel back into the UK when you're abroad and access any other local services. A VPN also protects your data, encrypting it, so you can browse with safety when you're away. ExpressVPN (www.expressvpn.com) is a good choice of VPN, supporting PC, Mac, iOS and Android, and it works with all UK streaming services. There's a free 30-day trial, so you can cancel your account if the service doesn't live up to your expectations without having to pay a penny.

Once you've registered an account you should download the client and install it on your computer or smartphone. From the app, you can then choose which country you want to appear in (the UK). Once the VPN has connected, all of your UK TV services should work.

Use the free CyberGhost VPN (less reliable)

You can use a free VPN service to try and watch UK TV when you're abroad, but these services can be a little slow and don't always work, with the BBC, in particular, blocking access to VPNs. Still, if you don't want to pay for a premium service, then trying the free option is a good starting point.

If you've got a Mac or a PC, you can use the free CyberGhost VPN software, which makes it appear as though your computer is located in the UK when it's really abroad. This will work for Sky Go, although the BBC has a regular crackdown on VPN software, so iPlayer may not work.

The downside is that the free version of the software isn't as fast as the paid-for premium version, and it can take a while to connect. For that reason, paying to upgrade your account might be worth it if you watch a lot of TV. Still, if you only want to watch the occasional programme, CyberGhost is a good choice.

To get it working, just download and install CyberGhost and then run the software. When it runs you'll get a pop-up ad asking if you want to upgrade, but you can just close this down and ignore it. Once the software has started, just click the big yellow button to get Cyberghost to automatically connect to the VPN. It can take a while to connect, and you may get a message telling you that there aren't enough free slots (Cyberghost reserves bandwidth for paying customers). However, we've never found Cyberghost to take more than a couple of minutes to connect.

Once Cyberghost has connected, it will automatically place your computer in a country. To change this and select America, click the menu underneath Simulated Country. Select the UK from the list and click OK, then click Reconnect on the next screen. Again, you'll have to wait for Cyberghost to find a free slot before it connects. Once it does, you'll see the map view update and your computer will be 'moved' to the UK.

Unfortunately, streaming TV providers are actively trying to spot the IP addresses used as endpoints by VPN services. This affects both paid-for and free VPNs and can make using them extremely unpredictable, as it's impossible to tell when they'll be detected.

If you like to travel light and don't plan on bringing a laptop with you when going abroad, there are still ways to tune in using a smartphone or tablet. VPN clients such as CyberGhost are available for Android and iOS, which can trick your mobile into thinking it's in another country. The Android version is currently free to use, but the iOS version requires a £25 annual subscription - if you're able to use less than 500MB of data per month the equally useful Tunnelbear is a free alternative for iPhone and iPad owners. Both run in the background on your device, letting you access websites and apps usually blocked based on your location.

With Android, you simply have to install the app and press start to spoof your IP address, but for iOS things are a little more complicated. Once your VPN app is installed, you have to head into Settings, tap VPN, then select the relevant name from the list displayed. With Tunnelbear, you should see a choice of "Tunnelbear UK", "Tunnelbear US" and any other servers you've selected through the app. Tap on the country you wish to spoof your IP address to and switch VPN to ON to start surfing or streaming.

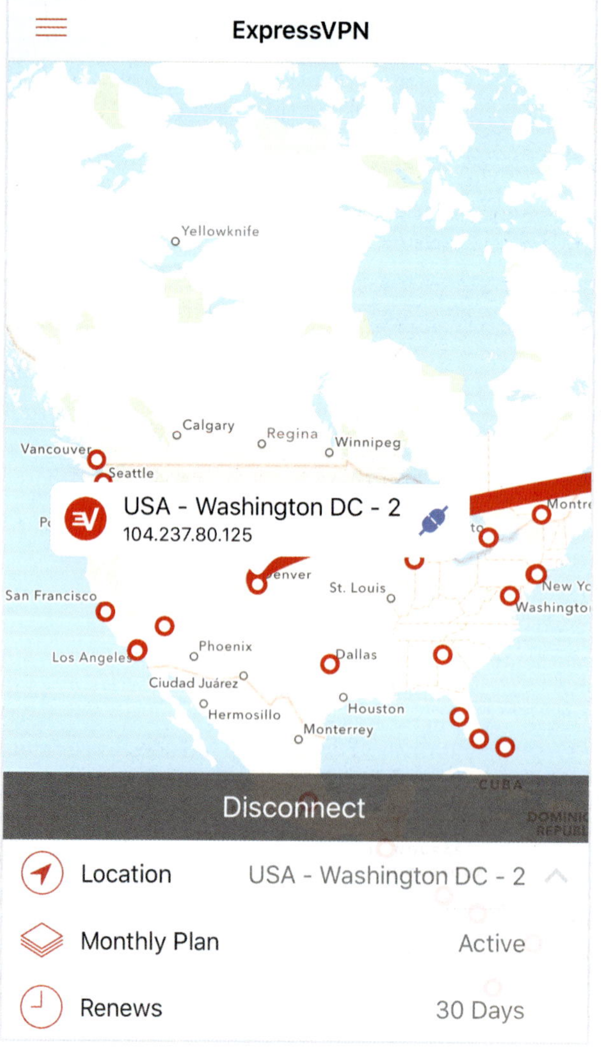

▲ You can use a VPN to watch whatever content you want.

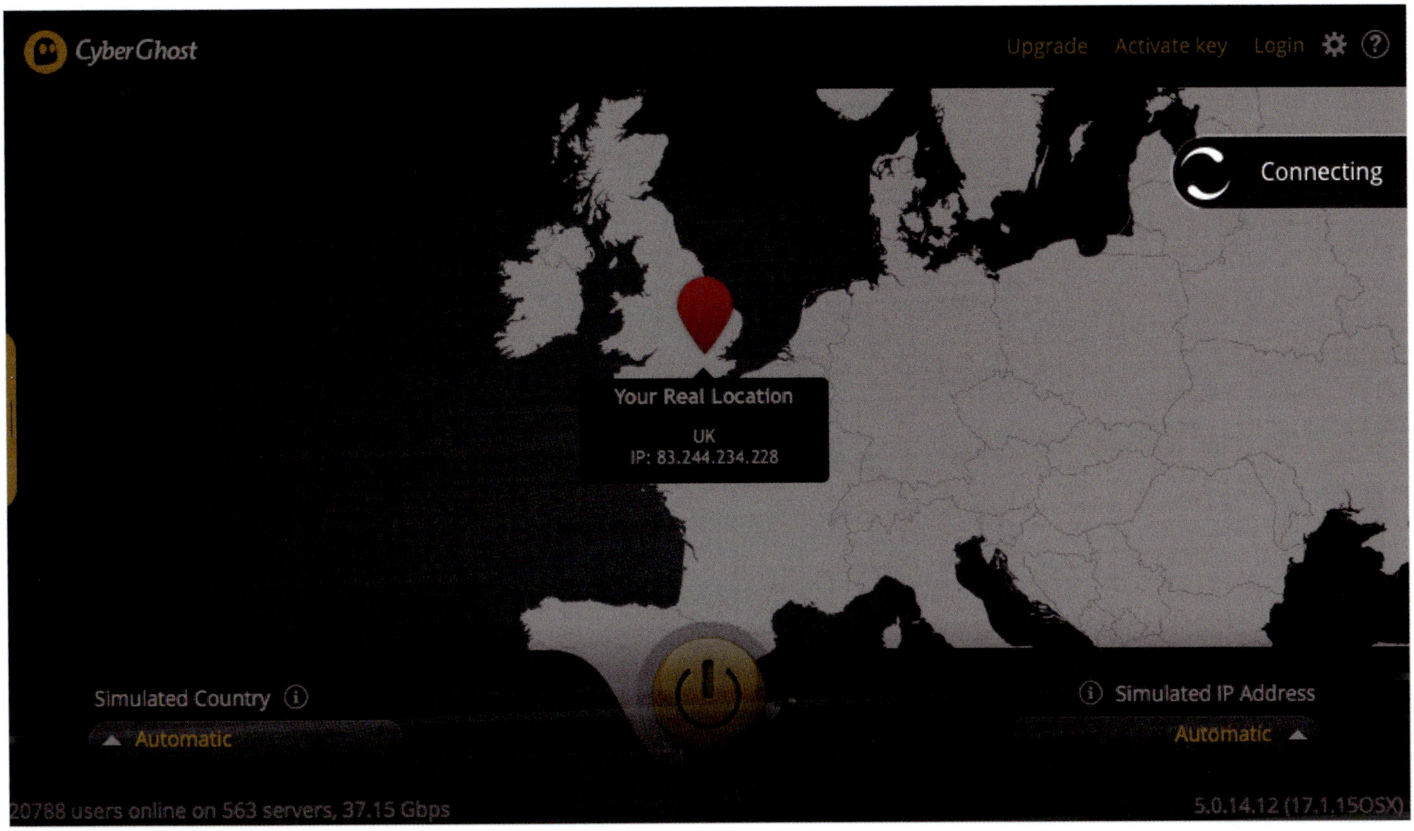

▲ Cyberghost is free and lets you watch a lot of UK services when abroad.

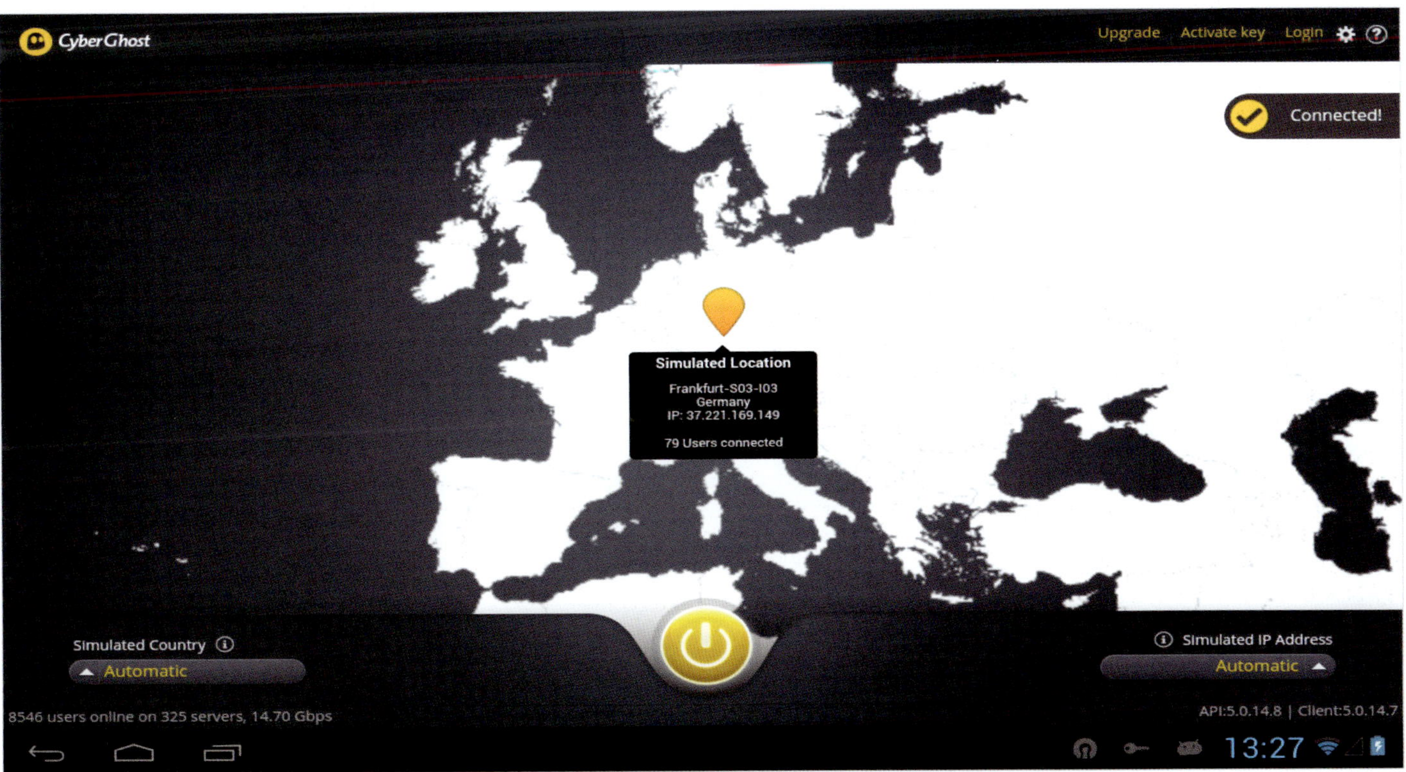

▲ CyberGhost has a free Android VPN app, too.

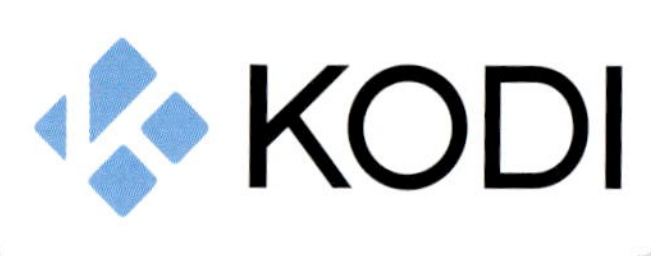

Download any video from the web

Torrents aren't all dubious, dangerous downloads – they have many clean and legal uses, too. We explain everything you've always wanted to know about BitTorrent

There are now more ways than ever to stream and download videos from the internet, but one of the easiest, no-cost options remains BitTorrent. The peer-to-peer file-sharing protocol has been allowing web users to grab movies, TV shows and other media files since 2001, and remains largely unchanged. Despite court orders making it harder to access torrent sites, ISPs throttling downloads and some BitTorrent software bundling nasty extras (uTorrent once included a sneaky Bitcoin-mining tool), torrenting is still very popular with an estimated 250 million users worldwide.

In this guide, we tell you everything you need to know about BitTorrent, including how to find and download any video you want; explain how it works and how to get the most from it; and reveal some of the best (and more unusual) BitTorrent clients.

What is BitTorrent?

BitTorrent, which was originally created by a programmer called Bram Cohen, is a peer-to-peer file-sharing method that

▲ The official BitTorrent client is to torrenting as a Hoover is to hoovering

▲ Much like football stickers, if you don't give with BitTorrent, you don't get

you can use to download pretty much anything, from music and videos to software and books.

All you need is a BitTorrent client. You can use either the official program (from www.bittorrent.com) or one of many other available alternatives – we'll list our favourites later. To begin downloading a file, you firstly need to find and download the torrent file or magnet link for it. A torrent is a small data file, with the logical extension '.torrent', which contains information about the item you want, including the name of the content, its length and how many parts it consists of. The torrent also contains the URL of the tracker – this is the host computer that coordinates the file sharing.

When you download a file from a website, you grab the whole thing from that one location. BitTorrent works differently and, instead, downloads separate pieces from all over the place. The file you want is divided into tiny data fragments, typically around 256KB each, and then shared among everyone who is downloading it.

The BitTorrent client reads the tiny torrent file or magnet link, connects to the relevant tracker and then, in turn, is connected to the 'swarm'. This is the name given to the group of computers sharing the file. The swarm is made up of 'seeds' (computers that have the complete download to share) and 'peers' (computers which have some of the file but are still downloading the rest). The larger the swarm, the faster the download will be.

BitTorrent only trades pieces with users who have something to give in return, much like swapping football stickers. You give a fellow sharer a piece of the data they want, and in return they give you some of the data you want. If they stop sharing the pieces with you, you stop sharing the pieces with them.

Rather than just downloading random bits here and there, the rarest parts of the file are prioritised to avoid the situation where everyone's downloads end up stuck at 99%.

The speed of your downloads is linked to the speed of your uploads – so if you throttle your upload rate, your downloads will also slow. Oddly, if you use your full upload capacity, that also slow your downloads a bit – we'll explain why later.

▲ Khaleesi won't be happy if she catches you downloading Game of Thrones

When BitTorrent first arrived, you needed a .torrent file to get the download you required, but in recent years magnet links have grown in popularity. These do the same thing as a .torrent file, but you don't need to download anything. Just click the magnet link and your BitTorrent client should spring into life and start the download.

Is torrenting legal?

Using BitTorrent is perfectly legal. It's simply a system for downloading and sharing large files over the internet. It's what you choose to download with the software that is potentially breaking the law. If you download copyright-free files, including classic and independent films, large open-source programs, and game demos; or files that are intended to be shared such as movie trailers, TV promos and funny videos, then you won't be breaking any laws. However, if you download a new blockbuster movie or the latest episode of Game of Thrones or The Walking Dead, that's a different matter entirely.

Is BitTorrent safe?

If you use common sense and stick to downloading torrent files from major (known) torrent sites, then you should be safe enough. Other users' comments and ratings should steer you away from any bad torrents, but that may not always be the case. There are certainly plenty of files that pretend to be something they're not. If you download a video file but it won't play because it claims you don't have the right codecs (software that's used for encoding or decoding a media file), for example, then it's probably not the movie you were hoping for, just a large fake file that's designed to trick you into downloading malware. Certain BitTorrent clients will let you steam videos as they download, which will help you avoid fully downloading a fake movie file. Be sure to scan the finished item with AV software.

Best legal uses for BitTorent

Torrents let you download videos without breaching copyright and potentially getting yourself in trouble. Here are our favourite legal uses

Download films from the Internet Archive

The Internet Archive has an extensive torrents section (bit.ly/archivebt399), which is home to nearly 16 million items from its collection. These include over 2.5 million items from the Moving Image Archive and more than 21,000 movies including full-length feature films, shorts, concerts movie trailers and home movies. Even if you only ever download torrents from here, you'll never be short of something interesting to watch. You can also download free classic and B-movie films from Public Domain Torrents (www.publicdomaintorrents.info) and get indie movies from Vodo (vodo.net).

Download legal 'bundles' of videos

In a bid to be seen as more than just a means to download illegal content, BitTorrent has started offering original and legal content in the form of bundles (bundles.bittorrent.com). These are a mixed selection of music and video – for example, Radiohead's Thom Yorke released a new album as a paid-for BitTorrent Bundle.

Chat privately with BitTorrent Bleep

Bleep (www.bleep.pm) is a peer-to-peer chat tool that lets you securely communicate with friends by text or voice. Unlike some 'secure' chat services, Bleep messages are fully encrypted from end to end and are only ever stored directly on your PC, Mac, Android or iOS device. No personally identifiable information is required to use it, and BitTorrent doesn't know who is calling who, or even when communications take place.

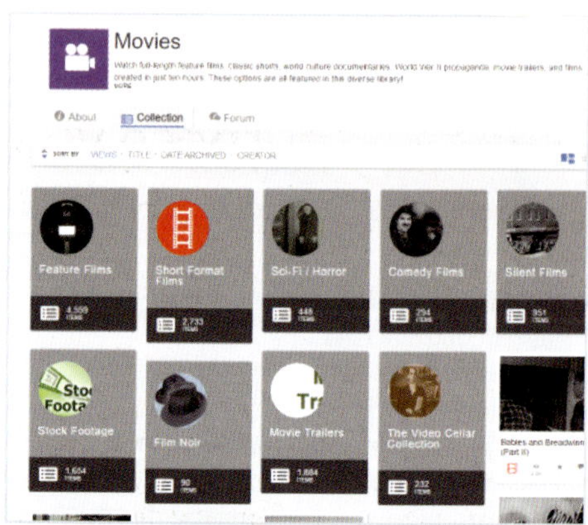

▲ Download millions of free and legal videos from the Internet Archive.

Find the best torrents using TorrentRover

No matter what you're looking for, this handy tool can help you get the best matches

1. Download TorrentRover

Before you start using TorrentRover you'll need to install a BitTorrent client such as Tixati (www.tixati.com/download) because the search tool can only find torrents, not download files. When done, install TorrentRover (www.torrentrover.com) and close the Get Prepared window. Enter what you're looking for in the quick search box and optionally choose a category to narrow results.

2. Start search

Hit the Go button and TorrentRover will search all of the popular torrent sites and display the results in the panel at the bottom. It will automatically order its findings by popularity, so the ones at the top will be the best ones to go for. To find out more about a torrent click the View Torrent(s) button.

3. Order the results

You can order the results by other categories, including site, age, size, number of seeders, number of leechers, ratio, and rating. Select one and click the blue arrow to download the torrent file. Once a torrent file has downloaded, your torrent client will spring into life and begin downloading the content, which can take a few hours to complete.

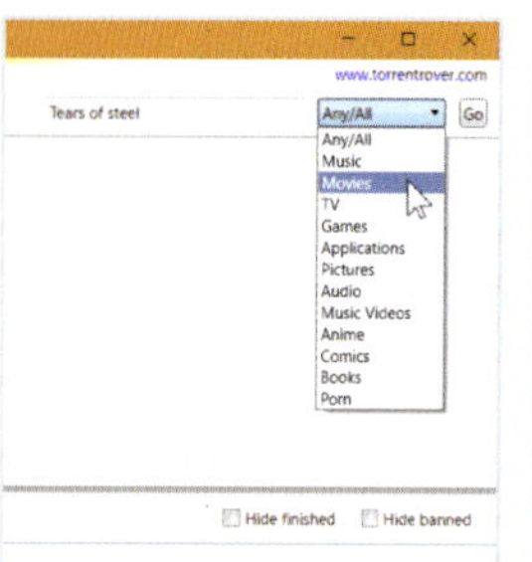

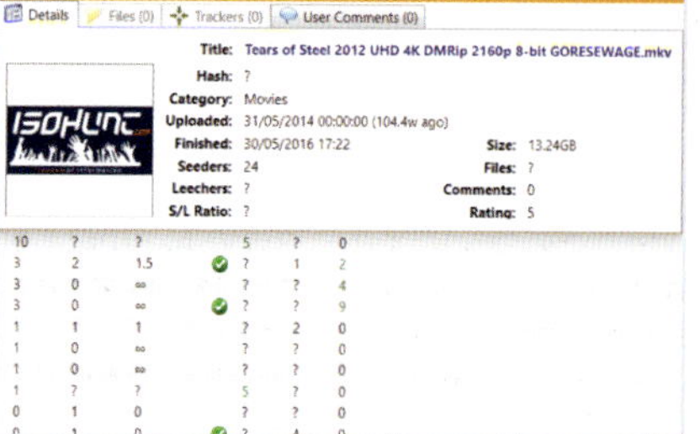

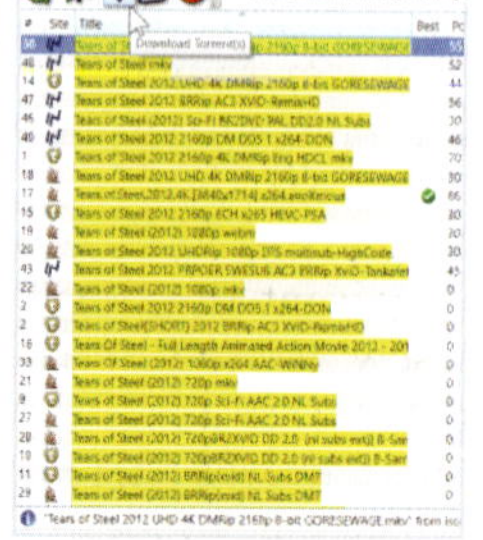

Essential BitTorrent tips

Whatever purpose you're using BitTorrent for, there are always ways you can download files faster and safely. Here are five of the most useful torrent tricks

Unblock banned torrent sites

It used to be very easy to download torrents from the web, but in recent years the courts have been clamping down on sites that link to them, and the likes of The Pirate Bay, KickassTorrents and TorrentBytes, are now blocked in the UK. Of course, there are plenty of other torrent sites you can track down using Google, but they may not be safe to use.

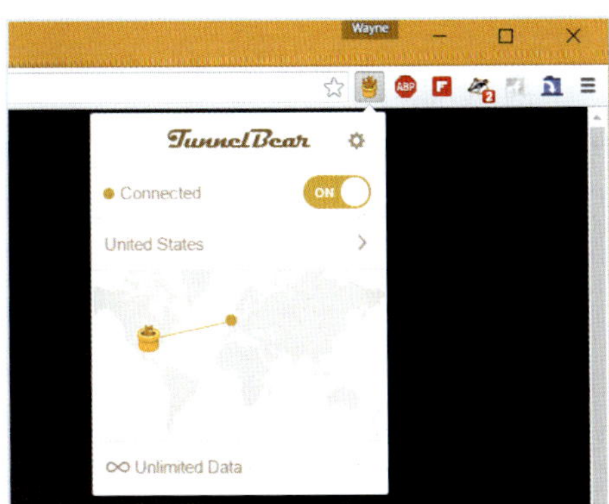

▲ You can use TunnelBear to access torrent sites that are banned in the UK.

If you prefer to stick with a well-known site, such as The Pirate Bay, you can get around the block by either using the proxy (there's a list at proxybay.one), or a free VPN tool such as TunnelBear (www.tunnelbear.com). Just remember that the free versions of VPNs limit the amount of data you can download every month, and video files can be massive.

Speed up your torrent downloads

The golden rule when using BitTorrent is 'the more you upload, the more you can download'. However, that's only true up to a point. If your uploads have reached a maximum, your download speeds will suffer due to the way TCP (Transmission Control Protocol) works. Use your BitTorrent client to limit your maximum upload speed to around 75%. Disguising your downloads so that your ISP doesn't know you're using BitTorrent can help, too.

Conceal your torrent traffic

Although they might deny it, many ISPs automatically throttle BitTorrent downloads, preventing you from getting the speeds you should. BitTorrent clients such as uTorrent (www.utorrent.com) can disguise BitTorrent traffic, making it less obvious to your ISP. To turn the feature on, go to Options, BitTorrent and select Enabled in the Outgoing box under Protocol Encryption. It's also worth changing the default port, which you can do in Options, Connection. Other BitTorrent clients offer similar options for disguising your traffic, so it's worth hunting around in their settings.

Avoid being a 'leech'

BitTorrent is about file 'sharing'. However, for every person who shares a file, there are multiple users who don't share anything. Referred to as leeches, all these users do is search for the item they want, download it and then move it elsewhere so no one can download it from them. This is, understandably, bad form. What should happen is that once you've finished downloading something, you become a seeder (a process that happens automatically). Seeders upload pieces of the finished file to peers with a fast upload speed and who can distribute them more effectively to other users. Although the BitTorrent system can function with just peers, so long as all of those peers have the full data set between them, seeders are essential to ensure any gaps that appear are quickly filled and essentially keep everything going. You should try to seed an item you've downloaded for at least a couple of days.

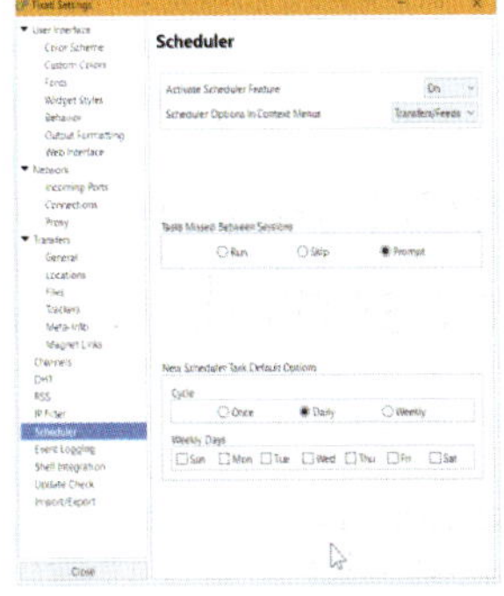

▲Schedule your BitTorrent downloads to take place at less busy times.

Schedule your downloads

It's a good idea to control when your downloads happen, because you can choose times when your internet connection is at its least congested - the middle of the night, for example - so speeds should be better. Most popular download tools include scheduling options. Tixati, in particular, has some very advanced scheduling settings to play around with. You should find the scheduling options you require under Settings or Preferences in your BitTorrent client.

The complete guide to TV streaming

With so much viewing choice these days, it's difficult to decide what to watch, where or how. We explain everything you need to know about streaming TV

It's fair to say that we live in a golden age of television. Long gone are the days of just three or four channels that closed down for the night and offered a heavy dose of repeats. Now not only are there hundreds of channels to pick from – depending on which TV platform(s) you have – the likes of Netflix and Amazon are muscling in with their own original programming, and seriously outspending traditional broadcasters.

Knowing what's available to watch, and what you need to be able to watch it (legally), is a nightmare. For example, while Roku and Apple TV give you access to the majority of streaming TV, a Fire TV device makes it easier to watch Amazon's growing raft of original content on the big screen. Even when you've decided which company to buy from, you may have to choose between a box and a stick.

Over the following four pages, we look at the software, apps, and services you might need. Read our guide on page 64 to find the best media streamer for you. We'll also look at the legal side of streaming TV, and reveal the best services for streaming TV.

▲ From comedy and drama to sport and documentaries, iPlayer has it all

Best services for streaming TV

Here, we'll go through the best TV services that you can get (free and paid-for), to help you find that one that matches your needs.

BBC iPlayer

www.bbc.co.uk/iplayer
You're probably very familiar with iPlayer, which lets you watch the BBC's channels live, and catch up with past programmes, and original – not yet broadcast – content. It's available as a program, on the web and as mobile apps for all the major platforms, and can also be found in streaming-media boxes such as Amazon Fire TV. You can stream content, download it, mark favourites and queue up programmes for later viewing.

Is it legal to stream TV?

It used to be you only needed a TV licence for watching live broadcasts. Catch-up and on-demand TV, viewed through the likes of iPlayer, was exempt, meaning if you never watched live programmes, then you didn't need a licence. However, the government has now closed this loophole. Now, you need a TV licence to watch anything on iPlayer. And this covers all devices – TVs, tablets, and mobiles. You will also need a licence to watch or record live broadcasts on any channel, not just the BBC. However, you don't need a licence if you only watch non-live streaming content from broadcasters other than the BBC, or movies and TV shows you've paid for.

▲ Catch-up on all of Channel 4's content, but be prepared for a lot of ads.

▲ It's better than it used to be, but ITV Hub lags behind the competition.

All 4

www.channel4.com/programmes/catchup

Unlike ITV Hub and My5, Channel 4's app offers Chromecast support and a huge free archive of classic series as well as live and on-demand streaming. However, be prepared to sit through lots of adverts before programmes start, and even in the middle - it's a bit like watching Channel 4 live, if we're being honest.

ITV Hub

www.itv.com/hub/itv

Better than it used to be, but still prone to crashes, rendered slow by adverts and lacking essential features such as offline viewing and Chromecast support. Still, if there was something on ITV that you really wanted to watch and had missed, this is your best route to catch up.

My5

www.my5.tv

My5 is Channel 5's on-demand hub. You can view through the website, or download the apps for Android or iOS, both of which now support Chromecast. There's no offline viewing feature at the moment, though, which is the only minor disappointment in a service that has been radically improved since launch. With plenty to watch and catch-up on, My5 is an essential site for UK TV viewers.

Netflix

www.netflix.com

Most people have heard of Netflix, and many will be subscribers. The service, which is available on all major platforms, offers an unrivalled selection of movies and TV shows, including plenty of original content, including House of Cards, Stranger Things, Orange is the New Black and Marvel's Daredevil. It costs from £5.99 a month (although the £7.49 standard plan offers greater value because you can stream to more than one screen, and in HD) and you can try it free for a month. There's even an £8.99 option, which lets you stream to four devices and includes a 4K option, too.

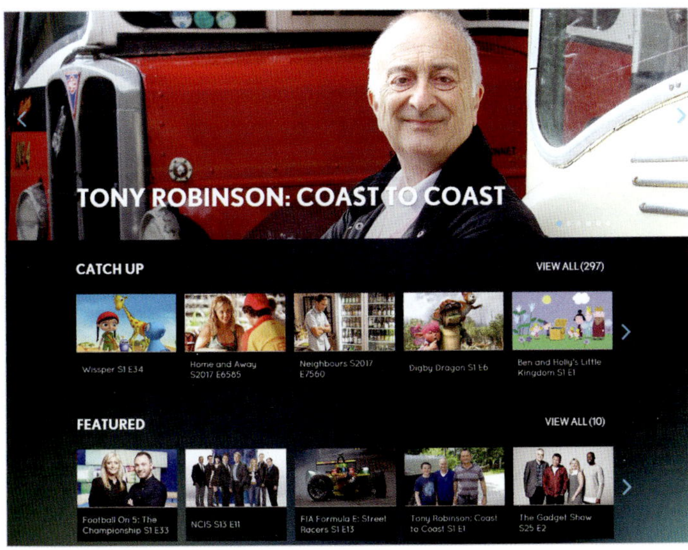

▲ bskufgskfugsiufgsi ugfis;ugf isgf

▲ With some excellent original series, Netflix is great value for money

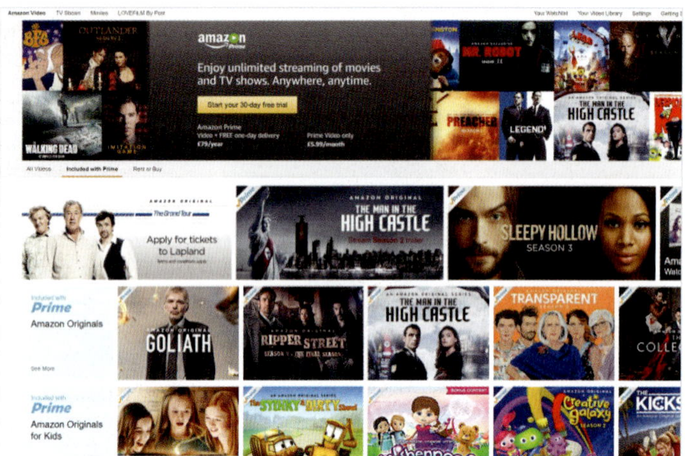

▲ You no longer need a full Prime subscription to stream Prime Video.

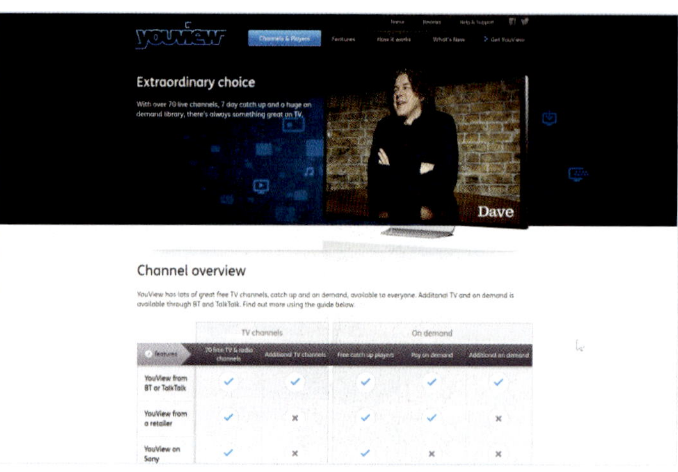

▲ There are lots of ways to get YouView and lots of channel to enjoy

Amazon Prime

www.amazon.co.uk

Amazon Prime costs £79 a year, or £7.99 a month (there's a 30-day free trial with all plans), but for that you get unlimited free next delivery, special deals, access to Prime Music and Prime Video, and more. Prime Video is available on Amazon's Fire streaming products, and also as mobile apps for Android and iOS. You can stream and download movies and TV programmes, as well as original Amazon content like The Man in the High Castle, Transparent and The Grand Tour. If you only want Prime Video, you can now sign up for just that for £5.99 a month.

YouView

www.youview.com

YouView is available as part of a BT, TalkTalk or Plusnet broadband package. There are also YouView set-top hard disk recorder boxes available to buy, priced from £160.

All versions of YouView offer 70 free TV and radio channels, including BBC, ITV, Channel 4 and Channel 5, and free catch-up TV. If you get the service from BT or TalkTalk you can get additional TV channels, including optional channels from Sky. YouView also lets you subscribe to Netflix and Now TV.

Now TV

www.nowtv.com

Now TV provides an easy way to access Sky content without being tied to an expensive subscription. You just buy the passes you require (Entertainment, Sky Cinema, Sky Sports and Kids) to watch live and catch-up content on your TV, computer, mobile phone or tablet, or a Now TV box.

Best free software for streaming TV

Turn your PC into the ultimate media centre using one of these excellent streaming programs

Kodi

kodi.tv

Formally called XBMC, Kodi is the perfect media centre software. It can play locally stored video and music files, stream web content, and if you have a TV tuner installed, you can watch and record live television. It's highly customisable too, following our advice.

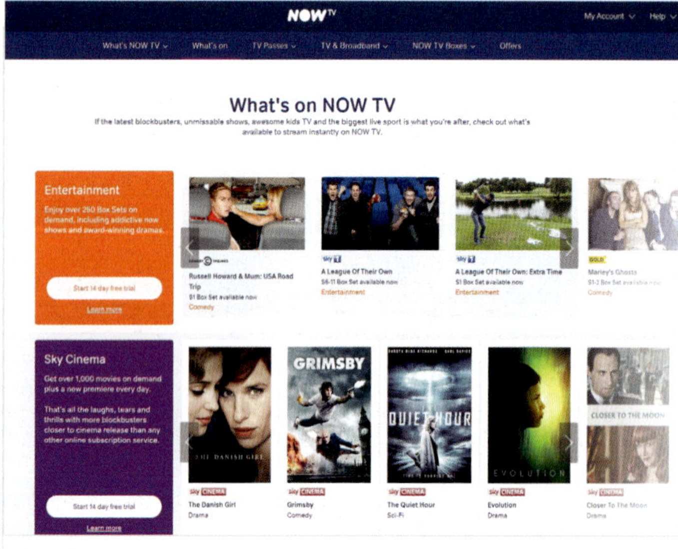

▲ Now TV provides a cheap and easy way to get Sky without a contract

▲ If you're not using Kodi to watch TV on your PC, you're missing out!

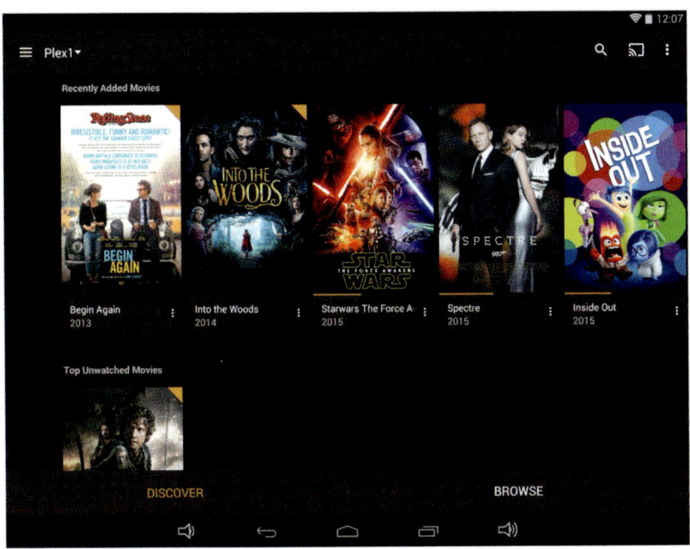

▲ Plex lets you stream all your TV shows and films to multiple devices

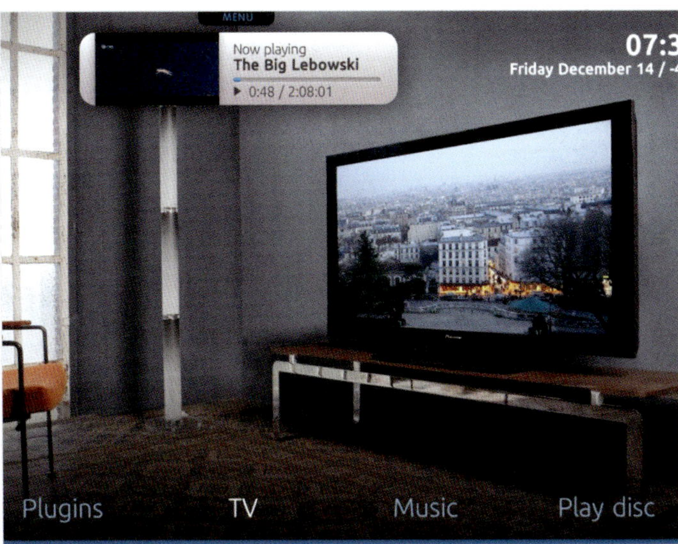

▲ The versatile MediaPortal offers much more than just video streaming

Plex

www.plex.tv

Plex Media Server is available for Windows 7 onwards, Mac, and Linux, and there are apps available for streaming to iOS, Android, Roku, Apple TV, Android TV, Xbox One/360, PlayStation 3 and 4, Chromecast and more. The idea is you store your media on a central repository, and then stream it to other connected devices. Plex is free to download and use, but certain features – such as recording from TV channels - are only available in the Premium version, which costs £3.99 per month

MediaPortal

www.team-mediaportal.com

MediaPortal is an attractive, easy to use media solution that, like Kodi, originated from XBMC, but has since undergone a lot of changes and improvements. It supports skins and plug-ins, and is straightforward to set up and configure. As well as playing local media, it can stream videos, act as a PVR, play radio and bring you the latest weather reports from your area. There are several versions and add-ons available, including aMPdroid for Android (bit.ly/ampdroid410), and the CouchPotato remote app for iPhone and iPad (www couchpotatoapp.net).

OpenElec

openelec.tv

Open Embedded Linux Entertainment Center (OpenELEC) is a small Linux-based OS that can turn your computer into a dedicated Kodi media centre. It can even be installed on a Raspberry Pi. As you'd expect, it offers the same functionality that Kodi does.

Windows Media Centre

Microsoft dropped Media Center from its latest operating system, but you can install it using WMC for Windows 10 which you can download from these Google Drive links – WMC 32-bit (bit.ly/wmc32-410) and WMC 64-bit (bit.ly/wmc64-410). Scan the downloads for malware before extracting the folder to your system drive (it should be clean) then open it. Right-click the file _TestRights.cmd and choose to 'Run as administrator', then right-click Installer.cmd and run that as an administrator, too. Exit when prompted. Windows Media Centre can do most of the basic tasks that Kodi can, but it's obviously a much older, less frequently updated program.

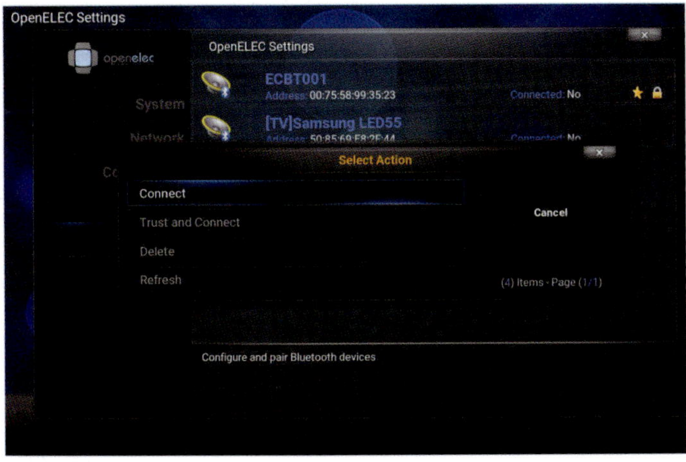

▲OpenElec lets you stream web video from your Raspberry Pi

▲ If you miss Windows Media Centre, there's a way to get it back

Stop the web blocking you

Websites seem to take a perverse amount of pleasure in blocking what you can see online. We explain how to beat these restrictions

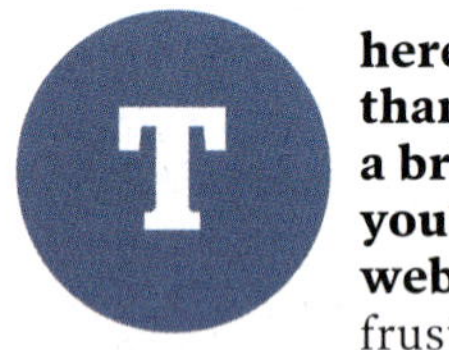

There's nothing worse than coming up against a brick wall when you're browsing the web. We've all been frustrated by videos "unavailable in your country", by ISPs blocking websites, and by warnings that "your IP address has been banned". Sadly, this is becoming increasingly common as web companies decide exactly what we can and can't access online. In this guide, we reveal how to beat the unfair blocks so that you can do whatever you want on the web without restriction or penalty.

Access banned download sites

From time to time, you might find Chrome and/or Firefox blocking access to popular torrenting sites. This happens when the site in question gets flagged as hosting potentially harmful programs or is branded as a "deceptive site" that may steal user information. This happens quite

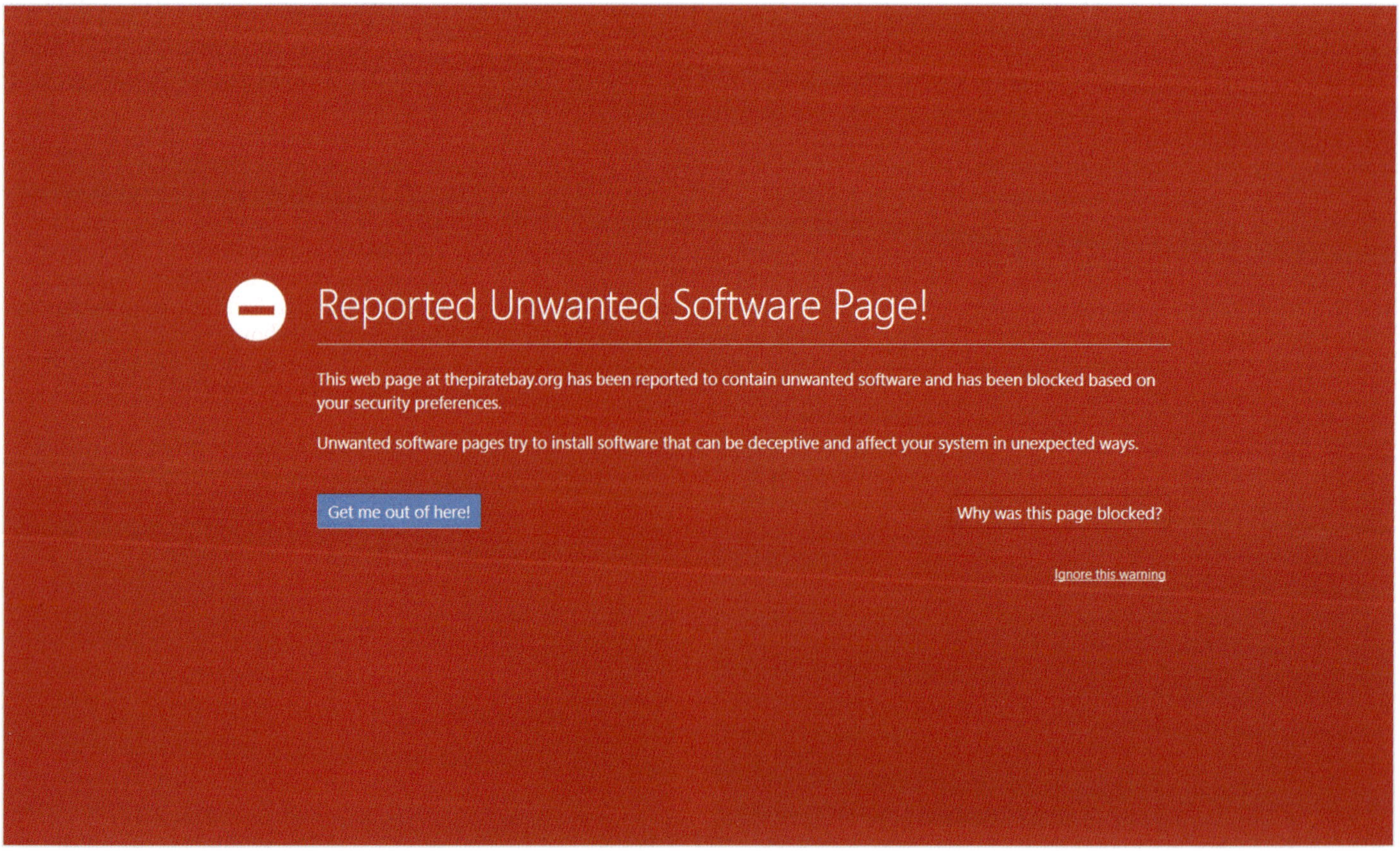

Reported Unwanted Software Page!

This web page at thepiratebay.org has been reported to contain unwanted software and has been blocked based on your security preferences.

Unwanted software pages try to install software that can be deceptive and affect your system in unexpected ways.

Get me out of here!

Why was this page blocked?

Ignore this warning

▲ Click 'Ignore this warning' to bypass Firefox's block on sites such as The Pirate Bay

▲ If YouTubeMP3-org is blocked, try FullRip.net instead

regularly – access to The Pirate Bay, for example, was blocked as recently as the first week in October.

Google's Safe Browsing technology is designed to keep you safe on the web, and is used in Chrome, Firefox and other browsers. When it determines a website to be unsafe, it will display a red warning page and block access to that site.

A browser block is usually only a temporary inconvenience. Wait a couple of days, and access should resume as normal, although you can get around the problem at any time. Firefox users should click 'Ignore this warning' to access the site (see screen grab), while Chrome users should click Details, then 'Visit this site'. Of course, it's possible the site in question might have been blocked for legitimate reasons – malicious advertising is usually the cause – so take care when bypassing the warning.

To beat an ISP block, try visiting the secure HTTPS version of a site – https://thepiratebay.org rather than http://thepiratebay.org, for example. If that doesn't work, then use a VPN to make it look as if you're browsing from outside the UK.

Use video-conversion sites

The video-conversion site YouTubeMP3-org (www.youtube-mp3.org) isn't currently blocked, but record labels are seeking a court order that will effectively put it out of business (read more at bit.ly/tube409). The site, which converts YouTube videos into MP3 files and which reportedly has over 60 million users every month, is accused of four counts of copyright infringement (direct, contributory, vicarious and inducement), as well as "circumvention of technological measures", which means breaking YouTube's rules on copyright.

The world's biggest record labels, including Universal, Sony, and Warner Bros, are behind the lawsuit, which is seeking $150,000 in compensation for every alleged act of piracy. It's asking a federal court in Los Angeles to stop web-hosting companies and online advertisers "facilitating" access to the site.

You can continue to use www.youtube-mp3.org at the moment, but it's probably only a matter of time before the lawsuit has an effect. If it is blocked, you can try other sites, such FullRip.net (www.fullrip.net, see image above), which lets you choose the quality of the MP3 audio (from 32kbps to 256kbps) and add ID3 tags to the track (such as song title, artist, genre, album, year, and track number).

Watch blocked TV in the UK

If you try to watch a video in the UK you may receive a message stating, "We're sorry. This video is not available in your region". You'll see this if, for example, you want to watch a free episode of one of HBO's series (http://www.hbo.com/watch-free-episodes). The broadcaster or the show's creators enforce this restriction usually because they don't have the rights to show the content outside of their home country (often the US for much of the current TV worth watching). Interestingly, it's often songs in

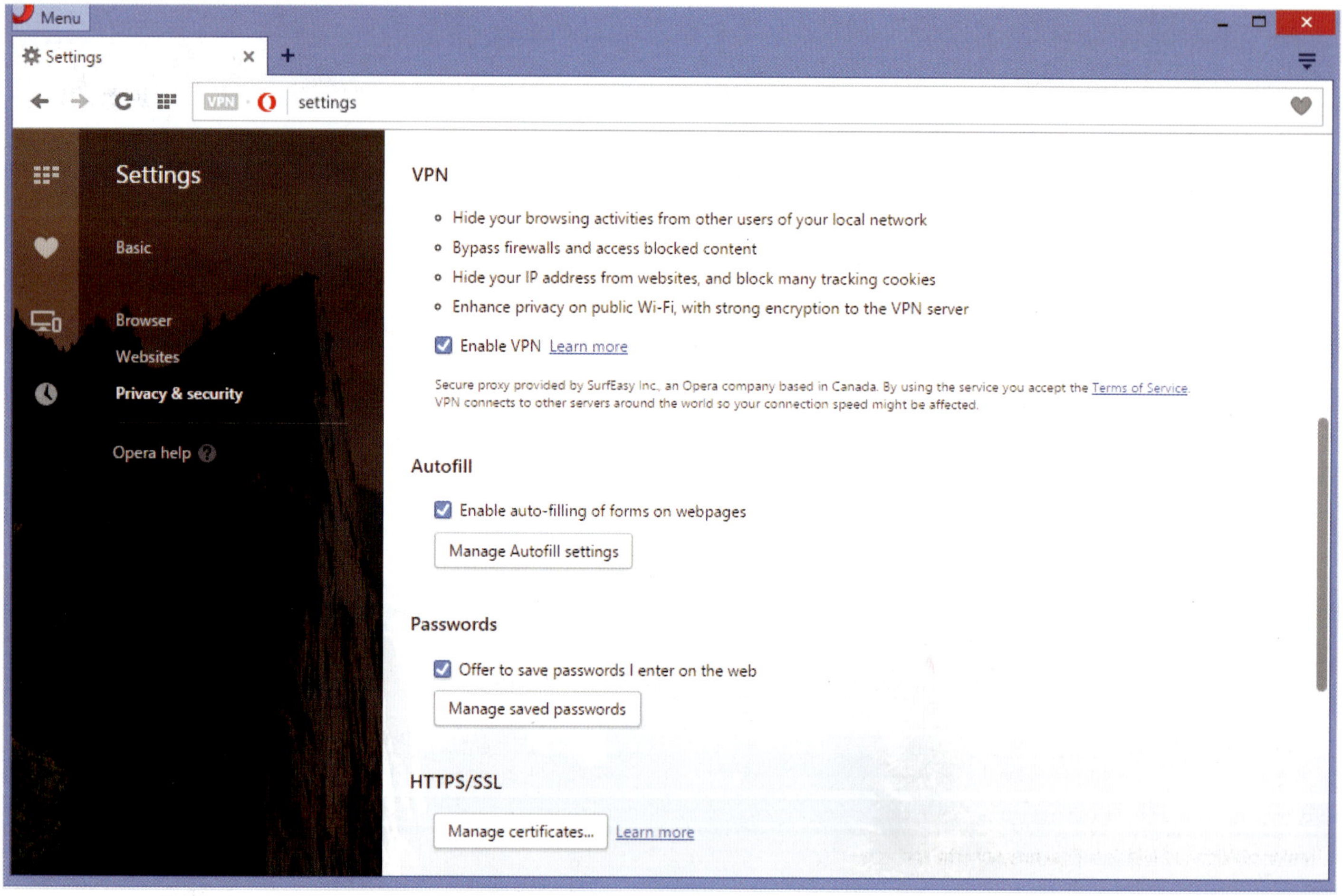

▲ Tick Opera's Enable VPN setting to watch TV shows blocked in the UK

the soundtrack that are the problem, not the actual video.

As always, a VPN is the easiest solution. The latest version of the Opera browser (www.opera.com) comes with a built-in VPN that you can use to get around the restriction. It lets you pretend to be browsing from the USA, Canada, Germany, Netherlands or Singapore.

You can enable the feature by clicking the Menu button, and opening Settings. Click the Privacy & security entry on the left and then tick Enable VPN (see screen grab). A blue VPN badge appears in the address bar. Click this and you can change the location. You might need to clear your browsing data before the video will play. Click the Clear browsing data button under Privacy & security and then refresh the video page.

Download Kodi and other streaming services

The child-safe filters ISPs use are also reportedly being used to block videos in the popular (and highly controversial) Kodi media player (https://kodi.tv/download), and other similar programs. If video doesn't load for you in Kodi, or its add-ons are failing to display lists, you might be a victim of these filters.

These filters are often enabled by default for new customers, and might be active without you knowing about it. If you're a Virgin Media customer, log in at bit.ly/vmsafe409 and deactivate the Child Safe filter. BT Broadband customers can see the instructions at bit.ly/btsafe409, while Sky customers should log into My Sky at bit.ly/mysky409.

Install mobile apps not launched in the UK

Developers don't always release new apps globally. Often they will test an app's popularity in one country only before choosing to release it in others. This happened in July 2016 when Pokemon Go was launched first in the US, Australia and New Zealand, leaving Brits watching impatiently from afar as the craze took hold.

The developer or publisher might block an app because they don't have certain rights for it overseas. Or, as was the case with Pokemon Go, an app's popularity may place too much strain on its server. The solution is to stagger the release across the world, so the app works as intended.

If you have an Android phone you could root it, although that's a risky option. Another option is to install Rocket VPN (bit.ly/rvpn409) to disguise your location. Launch the VPN and choose the country where the app you want is available. Google Play will be tied to your Google Account, and that will be linked to your home country, so you'll need to sign out of that, and create a new account based in the country with the app you want. You'll need to enter your phone number

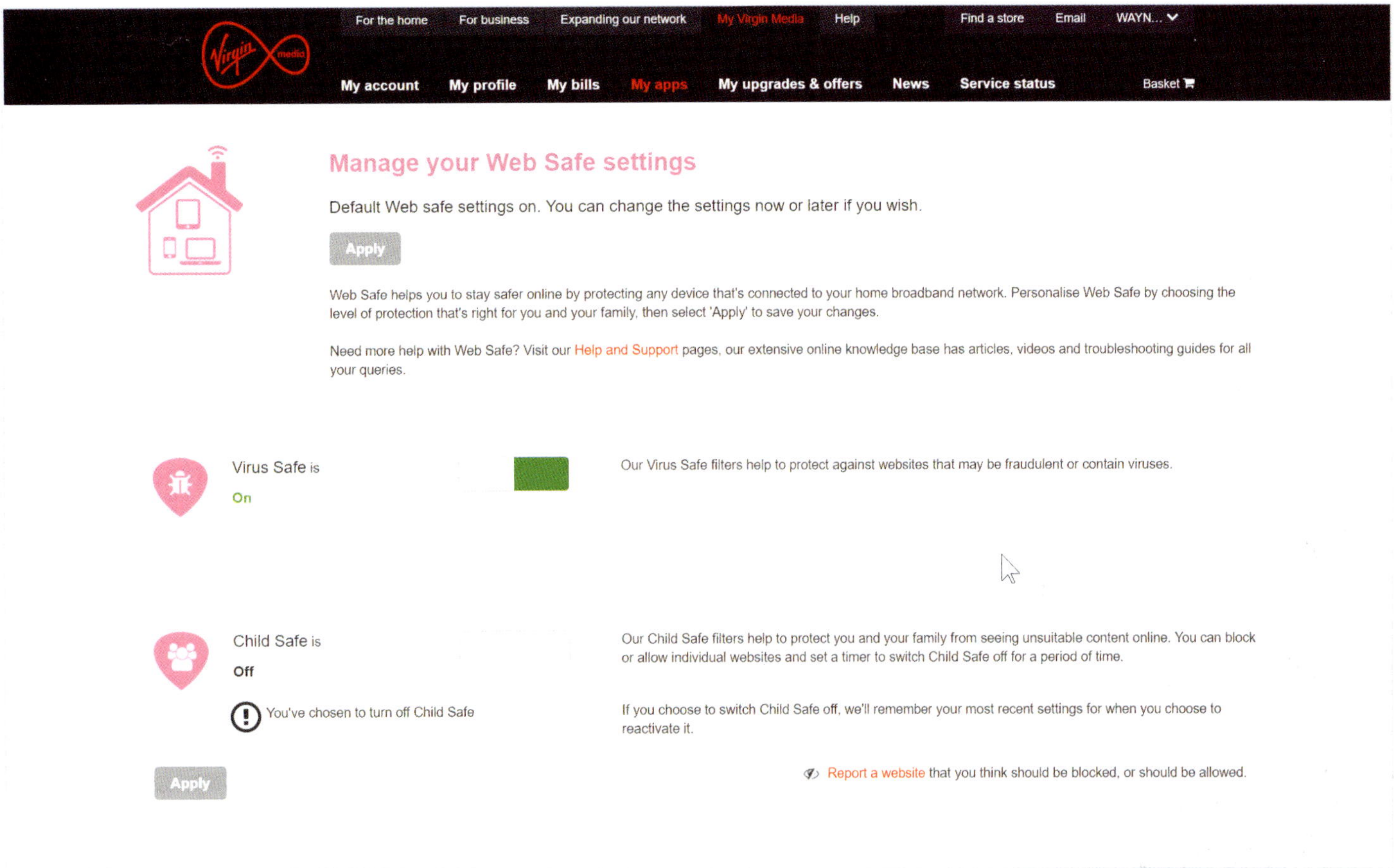

For the home
For business
Expanding our network
My Virgin Media
Help
Find a store
Email
WAYN...
My account
My profile
My bills
My apps
My upgrades & offers
News
Service status
Basket
Manage your Web Safe settings
Default Web safe settings on. You can change the settings now or later if you wish.
Apply
Web Safe helps you to stay safer online by protecting any device that's connected to your home broadband network. Personalise Web Safe by choosing the level of protection that's right for you and your family, then select 'Apply' to save your changes.
Need more help with Web Safe? Visit our Help and Support pages, our extensive online knowledge base has articles, videos and troubleshooting guides for all your queries.
Virus Safe is
On
Our Virus Safe filters help to protect against websites that may be fraudulent or contain viruses.
Child Safe is
Off
You've chosen to turn off Child Safe
Our Child Safe filters help to protect you and your family from seeing unsuitable content online. You can block or allow individual websites and set a timer to switch Child Safe off for a period of time.
If you choose to switch Child Safe off, we'll remember your most recent settings for when you choose to reactivate it.
Apply
Report a website that you think should be blocked, or should be allowed.

▲ Turning off Virgin's Child Safe filter may unblock Kodi content

for verification purposes, but the fact it's a UK number won't matter.

Afterwards, go to Settings, Apps, Google Play Store and tap Storage. Clear the app cache, then tap Force Stop. Search on Google for the app you want, then click the link to open it. Make sure the new Google account is the one connected to Google Play, and you should be able to download the app.

Rocket VPN is available for iOS (bit.ly/vpnios409), but it's harder to cheat Apple's system. You'll need to create a new Apple ID, and method of payment for the country you're choosing as your location (an iTunes gift card for that country will work). Changing your ID will wipe any existing subscriptions you might have through iOS.

Stop BBC iPlayer blocking VPNs

Like Netflix, the BBC is clamping down on VPN use, stopping users outside the UK from accessing its content for free. If you live overseas, or are holidaying abroad, using a VPN to keep up with your favourite BBC programmes seems like the perfect solution, but it breaks the corporation's terms of service. Last year, the Global Web Index (www.globalwebindex.net) claimed that more than 60 million people watched iPlayer content for free outside of the UK.

In response the BBC makes regular updates to iPlayer that block VPNs. It reportedly plans to launch a paid video service in America in the next few years, and so wants to limit what programmes can be watched beyond British shores.

iPlayer doesn't block all VPN services, so follow our advice on beating the block on page 82.

0MB
218 MB
∞
Left for this month
Get Unlimited NOW!
Connected to
United States
DISCONNECT
By using this application, you agree to our Terms and Conditions, which include anonymous traffic analysis and advertisement.
More details
Secured Connection

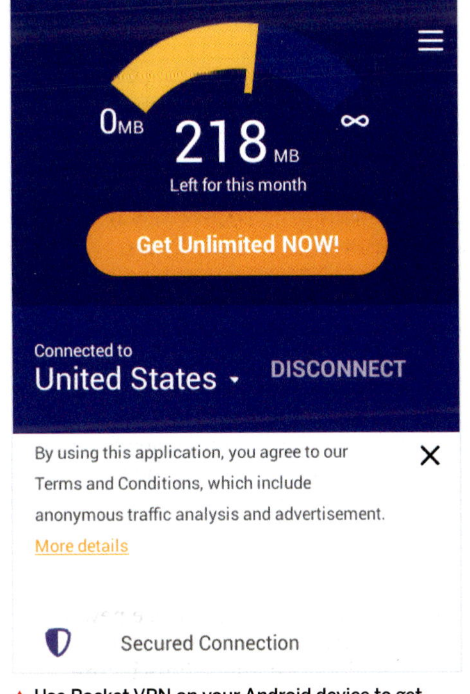

▲ Use Rocket VPN on your Android device to get apps before they launch in the UK

TunnelBear

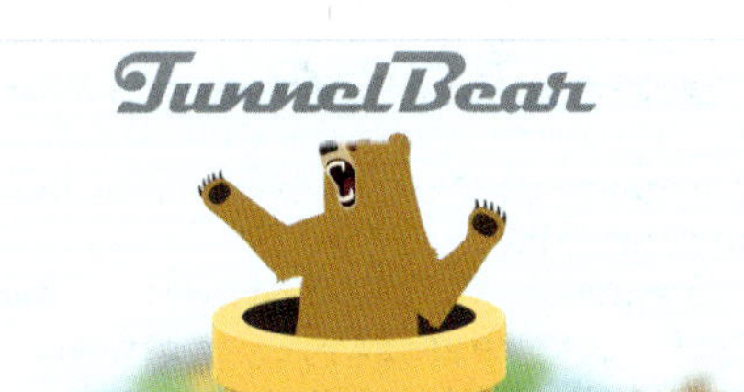

▲ The BBC updates iPlayer to block VPNs, but it hasn't managed to thwart the excellent TunnelBear.

How to watch Premier League football online legally

You can watch Sky Sports on your TV for free. We also explain how to use BT Sport and Sky Sports apps to watch on any device

Borrow a Sky Go or BT Sport account

If you know someone with a Sky subscription and they don't mind you pinching their Sky Go account then you can get Sky Sports, Sky Movies and other top channels such as Sky One and Sky Atlantic, along with Sky's excellent catch-up and on-demand service. If your friend has Sky Q, you can borrow their account details, although you'll need to use the newer Sky Q app to watch.

There is a device limit, however: Sky Go limits you to two devices per account on a standard account or, if you subscribe to Sky Go Extra, you can register up to four devices. This costs £5 extra on top of your Sky Go subscription. Sky Q supports four devices.

You can add and remove one device each calendar month, so if you're working with a friend on sharing your accounts, make sure you've both planned which devices you're going to be using.

BT Sport is slightly different: you can have an unlimited number of registered devices, but only two can be streaming at once.

▲ If you can borrow a friend's Sky account, you can watch content using the app.

Now TV

Another alternative (though unfortunately not free) is to use Sky's Now TV app for web browsers or Android and iOS with Chromecast. A Sky Sports Day Pass currently costs £6.99 and gives you unlimited access to Sky Sports for 24 hours.

Occasionally, Sky teams up with third parties such as beer companies to give beer drinkers free vouchers. Often these vouchers will end up on eBay for a fraction of their market value, so it's worth keeping an eye out for when these offers begin and buying vouchers in bulk.

▲ Now TV is a cheap way to get in on the latest sports action.

Supported apps for Sky Go and BT Sport

Web browsers

For Windows PCs, Sky Go supports Internet Explorer 8 and beyond and Firefox 3.5 and above. Google Chrome isn't officially supported due to the lack of Microsoft Silverlight support. BT Sport supports IE7 and above and an unspecified version of Firefox.

For Mac users, Sky Go supports Firefox 3.5 or above and Safari 4.0 or above. BT Sport only officially supports Safari 4.0 and above on OS X.

Mobile and tablet apps

Sky Go is supported on iOS 5.1.1 and above and Android 4.0 and above. BT Sport, meanwhile is supported on iOS 6.0 and above and Android 4.1 and above. You will likely run into issues if you're running "rooted" or "jailbroken" devices, however.

Games consoles

Sky Go currently supports Xbox 360, PlayStation 3, PlayStation 4. There's currently no support for Xbox One, however, so if that's your only option, see our guide below on how to watch on your TV without a compatible device. BT Sport currently doesn't support any games consoles.

Chromecast

BT Sport and Now TV support Google Chromecast.